# DON'T BLAME ME, IT'S EVERYBODY ELSE!

## (Continuing Adventures of a Confused Seventies Teenager)

By

Alex Cotton

For My Hubby

And They Said It Wouldn't Last!

# INTRODUCTION

After my second book, 'Don't Tell My Mum', people were still asking me what happened next. I originally intended to stop at the end of book one, 'Don't Look at Me in That Tone of Voice' but apparently, my family is so riveting that readers kept wanting to know what they got up to in the following years. All I can say is, you must be bored by now.

Anyway, I was persuaded to keep going so this book starts off again from 1977. I am now almost seventeen and engaged to be married, which sounds ridiculous now I know but there you go. I have almost escaped from the madhouse that I called the family home and am about to get a madhouse of my very own. My mother is both sorrowful at losing my board money and babysitting duties and ecstatic at the thought of buying a hat and being centre of attention at the wedding. My dad is still busy trying to pretend that none of it is actually happening and my brother doesn't really care one way or the other so long as he can eat beans at the reception!

So, once more. Off we go again, hope you enjoy it.

# CHAPTER ONE

## Long Lost Families

It was early December 1977 and almost my seventeenth birthday. For my birthday, this year I was getting an engagement ring and a party at a club in town. It was all very exciting. Well it was for everyone except for the two of us that were actually getting engaged.

From the moment we started planning it, the whole thing was hijacked by our families. It was to be done their way and that was that. We didn't really care, we just let them get on with it. As long as it came and went and meant that we could finally get away from all these nutters they could do what they liked.

At least we had picked my ring on our own. It was white gold and dead sparkly and was upstairs in the box ready for the party. When my mother saw it she wanted to know why I had only got a silver one and not gold. I told her it was white gold and actually more expensive but she just said people would think it was silver and assume I was marrying someone who couldn't afford a real gold one. Even now she was worrying about what people would think.

The actual wedding was ten months away yet and would be two months before my eighteenth birthday (see, I wasn't that young). Before that there was a lot of hoo haa to get through. My parents had to get together with his parents to plan things and that wasn't easy as they couldn't stand the sight of each other.

As I mentioned before, we had discovered that we had grown up a few streets away from each other and attended the same school even though we didn't remember each other. Because it was such a close-knit community it meant that our parents had crossed each other's paths over the years.

My mother had worked in some of the same factories as my future mother in law and despite faking delight in meeting again, they couldn't hide the horror and disgust in their eyes. My mother thought his mother was common and his mother thought my mother was stuck up (though I had to agree with her on that one). Meanwhile, my dad thought his dad wasn't good enough for our family and his dad thought exactly the same thing about mine. At least it meant we were never likely to all sit around the Christmas dinner table together.

Being the two-faced hypocrites that they were, they were nice as pie to each other's faces. Behind each other's backs though it was a different story. My mother could rant for an hour without drawing breath about the state of Sheila's perm and how many wrinkles she had on her orange face. My dad, meanwhile would be bending my ear about how that Frank was all show, putting on airs and graces when we all knew he had come from 'nowt', still had 'nowt' and would always have 'nowt'. While, across town at the other house, Sheila was poking fun at my mother's weight and dress sense and Frank was telling anyone who couldn't get away that it was about time my dad grew a pair and stood up to 'that battle axe'. I thought the fun would be never ending on the 'top' table at the wedding.

Our engagement party was being held in a German themed pub in the middle of town. It was a massive place with long benches that everyone stood on, singing German songs and waving big beer glasses filled with German beer. When it was in full swing it looked a bit like the Nuremberg Rallies. It was ever so sophisticated.

The reason it was being held there was because it was Frank and Sheila's favourite place in all the world (they hadn't been to Benidorm at this point). They had their own table (bench) there because they were regulars and they acted like royalty whenever they went in.

The place had various contests on the stage every week and would get members of the audience to come up and participate. One such contest was the Can Can, where half a dozen drunken women would get up and do the dance, flinging their legs as high as they could and flashing their knickers at the same time. Sheila was up there every week, flinging her legs around and flashing her stocking tops to all and sundry. It wasn't a pretty sight but it was better than watching her in the balloon contest. This usually consisted of the same women (it was always the same women) sitting on chairs on the stage with balloons between their legs. When the music started, they had to inflate the balloons by bumping their bums up and down on the seat of the chair. The first one to burst their balloon was the winner. It was always Sheila as she would wait until hers was big enough and then pop it with her cigarette end. She always had to win the contests or she would sulk for the rest of the night.

My dad had been to the club once before but my mother had never been and I couldn't imagine her standing on the benches slinging a massive stein of beer around. I certainly couldn't picture her doing the Can Can or humping a balloon on stage but who knew If there was a stage she usually had to be held back from getting up and entertaining (in her mind) the nation.

I was dreading it for two reasons. The first being my mother putting on an exhibition in front of people who didn't know her yet and the second being the fact that I was required to take to the stage myself. In there they had a tradition that, if you were getting engaged you were both called up on stage. The girl had to sit on the boy's knee while he sang 'If you were the only girl in the world' with everyone singing along and the German 'Oompah' band accompanying everyone.

We both knew it would be excruciating but at least we would be half drunk by then so we wouldn't care so much. Frank and Sheila had a word with the staff who promised they wouldn't get us up until the party was in full swing and we'd all had a few beers. For now, I was following my dad's example and pretending it wasn't happening. I didn't know why we had to have a big party anyway. I had only wanted a small one with my friends and cousins but once it was mentioned it just kept getting bigger. We should have been more assertive and just told them to stop.

My Aunty Dolly said she would buy us a nice present but she wouldn't be coming to the party as it wasn't really her cup of tea plus she couldn't trust herself near my mother when there was alcohol involved. She said she hoped I wasn't getting married just to escape from my mother, I assured her I wasn't and this was just an added bonus. The truth was we were both trying to escape our respective families. Mine were just nuts but his were complete whackos.

If ever any two people should have been sterilized at birth it was these two. They shouldn't have been left in charge of a budgie never mind three kids. They had a boy and two girls, Cheryl, my partner in crime in the cake shop, and an older sister Anne, who was married but secretly hated her husband. She really had only got married to get away from her parents and was now regretting it but daren't tell them.

It was Anne who had really brought the other two up. Frank and Sheila just got on with their own lives without really paying any attention to their offspring. They were brought up eating bread and jam and the odd bag of crisps with the occasional kit kat thrown in as a treat. Frank was of the opinion that you weren't allowed meat or fish until you were working and could afford to buy your own.

The kid's Sunday dinners consisted of lumpy mashed potatoes and cabbage, liberally sprinkled with salt, pepper and fag ash dropped in from the ever-present cigarette dangling from Sheila's ladylike lips. My childhood was strange but at least I never went hungry, even if my mother was no Delia Smith, plus she was a non-smoker so, until I had been for dinner at my in laws, I had never tasted fag ash.

They had only ever planned to have two children that they didn't want so when they realized they were expecting Cheryl it was a bit of a shock. Later on, they would laugh for hours, telling us about all the gin and hot baths and 'falls' down the stairs that had occurred when they were trying to get rid of her. It was nice for her to know how much she was cherished.

Frank also had quite a habit of pretending other people's children were his. If he saw what he thought were better behaved ones or better looking ones he would point them out to people as his own, ignoring the looks from his real offspring.

In front of other people Frank and Sheila tried to act like responsible, upstanding members of society and good parents. They were of the same school of thought as my dad, the most important thing in life was what other people thought. Because of this they told huge lies about themselves without a clue what they were talking about. One example was Sheila at a family party telling people about her weekly game of squash. Everyone started asking her questions about it (they all knew she was lying) while she dug herself deeper and deeper into the hole she had created for herself, trying desperately to change the subject. She didn't even know what squash was. The only weekly squash game she ever played was on a Saturday night, trying to squash her huge, man shaped feet into strappy high heeled sandals.

They also bragged about their holiday home in the country which was actually a caravan in a field outside town. It was only big enough for two so Frank and Sheila stayed in it while the three kids camped down in a nearby shed. I was really going upmarket joining this bunch.

But they were to be my future family so I did my best to get along with them. It wasn't that difficult really, I had a lifetime of experience dealing with the terminally deluded so I took it all in my stride.

For the next couple of weeks, I got on with picking my outfit for the party and making sure my friends would be there. If I had to spend a night with this lot I would need back up. I was cursing the day we had ever brought up the idea of a party. If I had known how they would all take over I would have kept my mouth shut.

Little did I know, I'd seen nothing yet. If I had thought they were hijacking the engagement I was in for an even bigger shock when they set their sights on planning the wedding. To this day, we both agree that the best thing we could have done was bugger off on our own to Gretna Green and saved everyone (including ourselves) a lot of bother.

# CHAPTER TWO

## Otherwise Engaged

It was the day we had been dreading for weeks. The engagement party. Most newly engaged couples would have been looking forward to such a special day but most newly engaged couples didn't have families like ours in tow. I arrived home from work that teatime and was ordered to eat as much as possible to soak up the alcohol that I would be consuming later. This was my mother's big rule about drinking. You would have thought she would have been more concerned about me drinking at all as I was still a year under age but I don't think that even occurred to her.

I shoveled down as many chips as I could manage and was then force fed a pint of milk to line my stomach, another of my mother's handy little drinking tips. She thought this would help if you were sick later on. It didn't. If you were unlucky enough to be vomiting the chips you had been forced to eat for tea, it was often made worse by the lumps of curdled milk exiting from your nose at the same time. I tried to point this out to her but she wouldn't give up and refused to let me into the bathroom to get ready until all the milk was gone. I felt like vomiting already before I even got near any drinks.

While I was getting ready in my room, my parents were also putting on their finery. My mother was heaving herself into her best dress, determined not to be outdone by Sheila, who, every week went out in various home-made evening dresses. A bit over the top for standing on beer soaked tables but there you go, I told you she was whacko.

Meanwhile, my dad was getting into his best (and only) suit. He looked like he was dreading the coming festivities even more than me. I couldn't blame him really, he was having to spend the next few hours with people who he detested and also had to keep a tight rein on my mother to stop her from attracting any unwanted attention. Never an easy task at the best of times. I think he was quite relieved that I was his only daughter and that he would only have to go through all this nonsense once.

Once we were all ready and my brother was settled with Joan from next door who was babysitting for the night, we set off. As it was a special occasion we were going by taxi instead of the usual bus. On the other side of town Frank and Sheila were boarding the bus, no such nonsense as taxis for them. Sheila was, as usual, treating the other passengers to the sight of one of her many evening dresses. She never seemed to notice the sniggers she got every week. The dresses were made by Frank, on his sewing machine, he fancied himself as a bit of a designer. His designs were definitely a one off, no other woman had dresses like Sheila, not that any of them would want one. She always topped them off with gaudy plastic jewelry and a massive fake fur coat. It was quite a picture.

We arrived at the pub around half past seven. Most of the guests were already there. Vicky had brought her boyfriend Derek, Melanie was with her boyfriend, Joe and Janice was there with a couple of her friends. She didn't have a boyfriend then but she was shortly to meet her future husband, Paul. Within a couple of years, we would all be married, even more amazingly, nearly forty years later we would all still be married to the same people.

Apart from a few other people, everyone else had been invited by Frank and Sheila. You would have thought it was their celebration, not ours. Just after we had been seated (benched), the doors flew open and Frank and Sheila swept in like the royalty they thought they were, waving grandly to everyone there. My intended was skulking along ten paces behind them trying to look as if he had never met these people in his life. Cheryl was behind him, dragging along her boyfriend Alistair who had somehow lost his shoe. Alistair was a dead ringer for Frank Spencer, both in looks and personality and Cheryl spent more time looking after him than anything else. They married shortly after us but were the only ones out of all of us to divorce some years later. Cheryl pulled the missing shoe from her handbag (nobody asked) and they sat down nearby.

Frank and Sheila were doing their usual meet and greet while my parents watched, open mouthed. My mother commented that Sheila looked like the world's oldest bridesmaid in 'that frock', while I begged her to keep quiet. As usual, once they met up it was all phony smiles and telling each other how nice they looked. My mother said how 'unusual' Sheila's plastic flower necklace was and Sheila asked my mother if she had lost weight. It was all very civilized, until they turned away from each other, both rolling their eyes.

One of Frank and Sheila's best friends was Barbara, who was the resident singer at the pub, she was up doing her turn when we arrived. I saw my mother watching her and I knew exactly what she was thinking,

"I could do better than that".  I was praying she wouldn't get the chance. After a few songs, Barbara came over to congratulate us and was introduced to my parents. After a bit of polite chit chat she said her goodbyes and went off to get ready for her next turn.

My mother watched her walk away and then put her foot right in it most spectacularly.

"It's a good act but you can tell straight away can't you"?  We all looked at her, puzzled, not sure what she was on about.

"Tell what"? I asked.

"That it's a man" said my mother. The penny dropped, my mother thought Barbara was a drag act.

Out of the corner of my eye I could see my dad trying his best to slide under the table and disappear from sight.

"Mother, she's not a man" I hissed, trying not to notice Sheila's clenched fists.

"Could have fooled me", came the reply.

Luckily (or not) we were saved from any further unpleasantness by the sound of our names being shouted over the microphone. Despite all the reassurances that we wouldn't be called on stage early they were dragging us both onto the stage before we'd even had time to order our first drink. This was turning into a nightmare.

The next ten minutes were all a blur. I was dimly aware of people cheering and singing, I was certain that I could hear my mother above everyone else. Apparently not even a German Oompah band could drown her out. Then it was over, the ring was on my finger and we were engaged. We climbed down from the stage to make way for the balloon humping contest and headed straight for the bar. What we really wanted to do was run away but people kept stopping us for a look at my ring.

Every time someone tried to have a look, my mother was at my elbow.

"Its white gold you know, not silver, its more expensive than yellow gold".

Dear god, why didn't she just hang a sign round my neck?

The rest of the night passed without incident really. Once my dad got a few of the massive lagers down him he didn't seem to care about people looking at him anymore and threw himself into standing on the benches, singing and waving his glass around with everyone else. My mother tried to join in as best she could but as she was so short it kept taking two people to get her up on the benches and as she didn't like the beer she stuck to martini and lemonade. I watched her waving a wine glass around, her head level with everyone else's elbows and thought she didn't really look part of the picture.

Thankfully, when the Can Can competition started she wasn't tempted to join in and was content to sit back and watch Sheila make a fool of herself while telling everyone within earshot that Sheila should really get those varicose veins looked at.

At last it was time to go home. We had posed for pictures, been bought drinks by complete strangers, dodged a couple of fights (not my mother and Sheila) and avoided being included in any more shenanigans on the stage. I was going home with my new family for the night so put my old one in the taxi and told them I would see them the next day. Ever the two-faced bitches, my old mother and my new one kissed each other on the cheek and laughed about how strange it was, after all these years that they were now related. They can't possibly have found it as strange as I did.

Back at Frank and Sheila's, we had a few more drinks, Sheila welcomed me to the family for the hundredth time that night and then we all went off to bed. I had to share a bed with Cheryl when I stayed at Frank and Sheila's house (no funny business under their roof except their own). Unfortunately, this night, Cheryl had drunk far too much and was hallucinating that she was on the big dipper roller coaster at Blackpool Pleasure Beach. Apparently, I was sharing her carriage. She kept screaming that she was at the top and was too scared to look down, then she would let rip with ear splitting shrieks, clutching onto me as (in her head) we hurtled down to the ground. Once down, the whole sorry business would start over as our carriage climbed back up to the top again.

After we had been on the big dipper for about twenty minutes, Sheila came bursting in and told Cheryl to get off it and go to sleep. She couldn't persuade her so we all had to play musical beds with my new fiancé drawing the short straw for the couch.

As I drifted off to sleep with the sound of shrieks, slaps and,

"Don't let me fall out, it's too high up here" ringing in my ears, it occurred to me that my new family was far stranger than my old one. Who would have thought it?

# CHAPTER THREE

## Too Many Cooks

On the following Monday I was back at work in the supermarket, showing off my ring to all the customers. It was a really small supermarket so we had the same customers day after day and we got used to all their little ways. Also, to some of their little smells. We kept a can of air freshener under the checkout for spraying around after some of the more soap challenged ones. All, in all we were a happy little band of souls. There were three of us girls, all the same age, the warehouse boy Wayne, two older ladies in their thirties who worked part time, the manager Mr. Burton and the deputy manageress Miss Turner. Miss Turner was the only fly in our ointment really, she was very active in the church and the boy's brigade and didn't find the world as amusing as the rest of us. She took her job far too seriously and was dreading the day (which can't have been far away) when she would have to retire.

She didn't take the news of my engagement very well, she said I was a silly young girl. Looking back now I can say she was probably right but back then I thought she was just jealous that she didn't have a white gold ring that looked like silver but which was actually more expensive than yellow gold. When she found out that I would be getting married in a church, even though I wasn't at all religious she was outraged. I told her it wasn't my idea but she didn't care, she told me I would pay for it one day. I wanted to tell her we were all chipping in to pay for it but I didn't bother seeing as she had no sense of humour.

I had quite a few duties at the shop. I was a till operator, shelf stacker, did stock control and also did some ordering. Recently I had been promoted to head (and only) cheese cutter. This meant that once a week I would be holed up in the back of the shop with my cheese wire and a mountain of different cheeses, all in big round slabs. It was my job to cut the cheese into loads of smaller pieces, then shrink wrap them, weigh them and lastly, label them and write the prices on them. After the first couple of weeks the novelty of this had completely worn off and I hated it. A lot of the cheeses were really wet and smelly and even when I wore an apron the smell would stay with me all day. I dreaded cheese day and was forever trying to get Mr. Burton to let me train someone else to do it. He would always say I was doing such a good job why bother.

In the end I gave up asking, anyway, at least it was better than my last job, juggling pigs innards and dodging pokes from my horrible boss.

What none of us knew at the time was that, within a few months my cheese wrapping, along with a bit of help from Miss Turner would land us all in a pickle.

For now, though, I was oblivious to what was to come and I enough on my plate anyway, planning my wedding. Or I should say, trying to, if only everyone else would stop trying to plan it for me.

The next couple of months were taken up with trying to convince everyone it should really be my choice of flowers, food, dresses etc., but it wasn't going well.

Firstly, there was the business of the guest list. My parents wanted to invite everybody they had ever met, or so it seemed. My mother came from a really big family so there were dozens and dozens of cousins and aunties and uncles, most of whom I had maybe met once when they came to look at me when I was born. I didn't want to invite any of them and I thought they probably wouldn't want to come anyway. All the weddings we had ever been to we didn't want to attend at all. We only ever went because my mother wanted to impress (or depress) everyone with her singing.

At Frank and Sheila's, it was the same story. They wanted all their long-lost relatives to be there, along with every old friend they'd never liked. It was ridiculous. By the time both sets of parents were finished, they had crossed most of our friends off the list to make room for all theirs. They graciously said we could invite them to the night time disco though so that was alright.

My mother was in charge of the cake. That didn't mean she was making it, thank god. Readers of previous books will know about how 'famous' she was for her baking skills, or rather, infamous. No, she was in charge of finding the nicest one that was also the cheapest one. She found a lady on our estate who made nice ones so a deposit was paid and that was one thing crossed off the list. I hated fruit cake but my mother said if I asked for a sponge one people would be talking about us for years. I thought they would probably have far more important things to talk about but what did I know?

The one thing I was sticking firm to was my bridesmaids Vicky and Melanie. Frank and Sheila were suggesting various cousins on their side but I didn't know any of them.

Besides, bridesmaids were my department and I wanted my best friends there on the day. The way things were going they might be the only people there who I recognized. I made a compromise and let Frank and Sheila sneak one little cousin in who was only five and who I had met a few times.

The other thing I was adamant about was the actual bridesmaid's dresses. Frank was determined to get out his sewing machine and make them himself. I told him the dresses would be picked my me and my friends and Vicky and Melanie were right behind me on this. In fact, they were threatening to jump ship if I brought anything Frank made anywhere near them. They had seen what Sheila was wearing at my engagement party and that had frightened the life out of them.

I assured them that they would be safe and just to get Frank distracted I said he could make a dress for the little bridesmaid. She was dead excited just to be a bridesmaid so I didn't think she'd care that much as long as she had a long dress to twirl about in. By the time she got older and looked back at the photos it would be too late for her to complain about how hideous she looked. Anyway, I'd had to suffer as a hideous bridesmaid in my younger days so why shouldn't she. I figured it was a rite of passage that we all had to go through.

For about five minutes my mother toyed with the idea of getting my little brother to be a page boy but she soon went off the idea. She knew from bitter experience that he would flatly refuse to do anything he didn't want to. It was still bad enough just trying to get him to school every morning and she didn't think the sight of him being dragged down the aisle by his legs would go down well with the congregation.

He was eight years old now and still mostly existing on a diet of baked beans. Recently my mother had succeeded in getting him to eat sausages with his beans but only if they were skinless. This had proved a major embarrassment for me when I took him with me one day to meet my in laws to be. Firstly, they asked him if he wanted a cup of tea, he told them he only drank PG Tips, then they asked if he wanted to stay for tea and he told them only if they had skinless sausages and Heinz beans.

This was the couple who only fed their own kids if they really had to, and then only with the cheapest rubbish they could find. They had never met anyone like him. I had given him a swift kick under the table and vowed never to take him anywhere ever again. After that little encounter, they called him 'Little Lord Fauntleroy' for the next ten years.

As if we didn't have the madness of the wedding to deal with we also had to find somewhere to live after the wedding. We couldn't get a mortgage as I was too young and both of us hadn't been in steady jobs for long enough so we would have to find somewhere to rent.

We were in no rush to find anything, we figured everything would just fall into place and we still had a few months yet, we were so naive it was unreal. We should have been a bit more on the ball as eventually Frank and Sheila took that upon themselves as well.

We only had ourselves to blame.

# CHAPTER FOUR

## Pork Pie and Pickles

It was now half way through May and the wedding of the year (in our house anyway) was only four months away. I was trying not to think about it as by now it really was nothing to do with either of us, all that was required of us was that we show up on the day and do whatever the vicar told us. Both families had to have a meeting with the vicar when we booked the church and the meeting had taken place at Frank and Sheila's house a few months before.

We all gathered in the living room to drink tea (still not PG Tips) and talk about ourselves. Frank immediately started telling a pack of lies about his life while my dad sat open mouthed. He had always reinvented his life in his head, changing it as he went along to better suit himself but he had never met anyone else who did it so blatantly and over the top.

Besides, when he did it he actually believed it, as far as he could see, Frank was just telling lies to look important. I was used to it by now so I thought nothing of it. Anyway, a lot of people who lived in council houses had a yacht in the marina didn't they?

When it came time to fill in the forms it got interesting. The marriage certificate required both father's full names and occupations, which brought back memories for my mother of when she and my dad had done that twenty odd years before. This was the time when my Nanna's little dark secret had surfaced and everyone found out my dad's dad wasn't really his dad and in fact the poor man had died nine years before my dad was born.

There really was no need to tell the vicar about this at all, and certainly no need to tell him how my poor Nanna had 'been a right slut behind everyone's back, while pointing the finger at everyone else'. I thought my dad was going to have a stroke. I knew from past experience it would be a very quiet bus ride home, followed by a blazing, whispered row in the kitchen.

I was secretly hoping the vicar would say that he couldn't possibly marry such heathens in his church what with me being descended from such debauchery but just my luck he really believed in all that forgiveness malarkey and said he would see us in church. He did leave really quickly after that though, he left half of his tea.

Half an hour later me and my parents also left to start the journey home in stony silence. I wished I had normal parents who would just have an argument and get it over with. It was going to be a long night.

Back at work next day things were about to take a turn for the worse, this was the matter of the cheese and Miss Turner.

It was a quiet afternoon in the shop, I was stocking the shelves with tins of soup and watching the clock, counting down the hours until I could go home. That night we were going to see John Travolta in Saturday Night Fever and I was looking forward to it.

Suddenly I noticed Miss Turner following an old man up and down the aisle. I knew what she was up to, she fancied herself as a bit of a store detective on the quiet and was forever following people she was convinced were shop lifting. Mr. Burton had asked her to stop on numerous occasions as we had been getting a few complaints but she thought it was her civic duty and kept on doing it.

On this occasion though, her suspicions were correct. She spotted this old man picking things up and putting them in his pocket. She needed to write a list of these things down for evidence but she had no notepaper. The only thing she had to hand was a large box that had contained Andrex toilet rolls, it was about three feet in length but she took it anyway and started writing a list of the things he was stealing.

It was a short list. The only things he took were a small pork pie and a piece of cheese labelled by yours truly. I would have turned a blind eye, he was old and maybe he couldn't afford the food. Miss Turner didn't care about that, as far as she was concerned he was breaking one of the commandments. This was the chance she had been waiting for. She ran and got Mr. Burton and told him if the poor old man left the shop without paying for the things he was to go out and grab him.

Poor Mr. Burton sighed, rolled his eyes but did as she asked, he only ever wanted a quiet life with the chance to nip out and play a round of golf if we were having a slack day. We all used to cover for him on these days if head office called. Well, all of us except Miss Turner who thought it was a mortal sin to tell a lie.

Anyway, the old man went through the till and only paid for a tin of peas, the pork pie and bit of cheese remained in his pocket. As soon as he left, Mr. Burton followed him out and challenged him. He made him empty his pockets and give back the loot, which only came to 95 pence for the lot. It was hardly the haul of the century.

Mr. Burton would have left it at that and just given the man a warning but it was too late for that. Miss Turner had already been on the phone and called the police and they arrived a few minutes later. They responded to any old rubbish in those days, not like today when they only come if you're being murdered and only then if they're not too busy that day catching speeding motorists to pay for the Christmas party.

They took the man back inside for questioning and before we knew what was happening they had taken him off to the police station along with the pork pie, piece of cheese and the cardboard toilet roll box for evidence. It was madness.

We all felt really sorry for the poor old man but Miss Turner was acting all righteous and smug. She kept saying,

"Thou Shalt Not Steal", and then she took herself off to gloat in the back room.

I thought about Jesus feeding the poor and the hungry, this didn't seem to occur to her even though she was forever reading the bible. It didn't seem very Christian to me.

We all went back to work and got on with the rest of the day. If we thought that was the end of it though we were very much mistaken.

I tried to put it out of my head and that night me and my husband in waiting took ourselves off to the cinema to watch Saturday Night Fever. In those days, you got two films for your money, they always showed a cheaper made B movie first. This meant you were in the cinema for about four hours.

That was always a problem for my intended as he had a bladder the size of a peanut. He would be up and down every half hour to go for a wee and could never find his way back to his seat in the dark. He would blunder around in the darkness, sitting on unsuspecting people's knees until I would rescue him and drag him back to his seat.

Over the years his bladder never got any bigger, he was always disappearing, looking for somewhere to wee. It could be especially embarrassing for him if we were in a pub. As fast as he drank something he would need to get rid of it so after every drink he would get up and go to the gents. He said once he had been in there so many times that night that he thought the other customers must think he was a pervert.

We made it through the first film then after he had been off for a wee and we had bought ice creams we settled down to watch Saturday Night Fever at last. I was really enjoying it until he started fidgeting around and nudging me. When I asked him lovingly what the bleeding hell he thought he was doing he whispered in my ear.

"When does Olivia Newton John come on"? He thought he was watching Grease.

He never did listen to a word I said, even back then.

The next day back at work I was discussing the film with my friend Debbie in the warehouse. She had seen it the week before and loved it. We were practicing the hustle round the stacks of self-raising flour when Wayne shouted that the police were back and they wanted to talk to me. Now what?

I was called into the tea room which was really only the size of a large cupboard and the policeman from the day before was there along with a detective in plain clothes. The detective asked me to sit down and then produced the piece of cheese which had been taken off as evidence. He started by asking me if I recognized it. I said yes, I had wrapped and labelled it. Then he asked me if the writing on the label was mine, again I said yes.

"Look carefully now, we don't want any mistakes" he said. "Is this definitely your writing"?

"Yes" I said again, there was nothing else to say.

"Just to be absolutely clear, is that the cheese that you wrapped and labelled, and is that your writing on the label"?

I was starting to get a bit worried now, he was treating me like I was a criminal.

"Yes".

"Are you certain about that"?

"Yes".

If this had been a few years later I would have been expecting Jeremy Beadle to pop up from behind the freezers, telling me I had been set up while everybody else fell about laughing. That was what it felt like.

The detective seemed satisfied at last. Then he told me that he had to make me see what it felt like to be interrogated like that because that's what would probably happen when I got to court.

"What, who said anything about going to court"?

He explained that the poor old man who had been caught red handed shoplifting had decided to plead not guilty and his case was going to Crown Court to be heard by a judge. Me and Mr. Burton and Miss Turner would have to go and be witnesses.

This was proper court like on the telly where the judge and the barristers all wore gowns and funny wigs. All that performance for a pork pie and a bit of cheese. It was ridiculous.

The court date was set for two weeks later and would probably last for a week. Even worse, it was being held in the next town instead of in ours. We would have to be off work for a week and trail there every day.

Mr. Burton was furious, I'd never seen him mad before. He wasn't mad with me, just Miss Turner. Because of her playing store detective, extra staff would have to be brought in for the week, we would all be stuck in a car together driving backwards and forwards to another town every day and worst of all, Mr. Burton wouldn't be able to sneak away for a quick round of golf. Miss Turner had dropped us well and truly in it.

When I got home that night and told my mother she was furious. Nobody from our family had ever been in court before. She was mortified she said. I pointed out to her that it wasn't me in the dock, I was only there as a witness but she said that's how rumours got started. Someone would see me going in there and before you knew it half the street would be talking about us.

I didn't think it was very likely as we didn't know anyone in the town I would be going to but she wouldn't be calmed down. She said she would write a note to get me out of going, I reminded her that we were talking about Crown Court, not P.E. Her last word on the subject before she broke the news to my dad was,

"Trust you to bring this on us".

Good god, what would she do if I really was the one in the dock? Probably hang herself because of the shame or disown me, or both.

I consoled myself with the thought that in another few months I would be free from all this madness. I could do what I wanted and never care what the neighbours might think ever again. I even thought for a minute that I might take up shoplifting, just to watch my mother try and explain that one away when I was in the papers. I thought better of it though, I would need more than just a pork pie and a bit of cheese and if you had to go to Crown Court just for that I would probably end up doing ten years hard labour. It probably wasn't worth the effort.

# CHAPTER FIVE

## Those Sleeves aren't Puffed

The next week I had wangled a Saturday off by switching my day off with one of the other girls so me and Vicky and Melanie went off into town to pick out the bridesmaids' outfits. They both wanted something simple so we looked around for a bit and then found the perfect dresses. They weren't traditional bridesmaid's dresses, just long cream cotton dresses with small flowers on them and short sleeves with a bit of nice trim. They were really just long summer frocks but they fitted really nice and we all liked them.

In another shop, we found some nice summery straw hats with a couple of small flowers in the brim which matched the dresses. They looked like the perfect outfits. All we needed now were the shoes to go with them. It was all too easy, in the next shoe shop we found some sandals which went with everything else. We had found the perfect outfits and it hadn't even been hard. We celebrated by going for patty and chips at our old favourite place in the market, the stripy red and white tent with the sawdust on the floor.

We might be a bit older but we were still as classy.

I wished it had been as easy getting my wedding dress. I had tried on a few that were within our budget and didn't really like any of them that much. I picked the best of the bunch but I didn't like it. It was high necked with long lace sleeves and a train. I had a small veil to go with it and a flowery head dress. It wasn't 'me' and I didn't feel comfortable in it but never mind, it was long and white and would do the job.

By this time, the wedding had become the Frank and Sheila show. Even my parents had been pushed out now, everything was being organised by these two. The photos were being done on the cheap by Frank's brother with the camera he had got for Christmas, the flowers were being done by Frank and Sheila's gay best friend Terence and the catering was being sorted by Marjorie who was Terence's wife (he was still in the closet at this point but the door was almost hanging off its hinges). I think Marjorie was the only one who still didn't know.

When I told them about the bridesmaid's dresses Frank said he would need to see them so he could colour coordinate the little bridesmaid's dress. I took one of them round to show him. Straight away he said that they weren't proper bridesmaid's dresses, they weren't even shiny and where were the puffy sleeves? I told them my friends were eighteen, not eight and this is what they were wearing.

Frank examined the dress and said he would pick up one of the colours in the flowered pattern and make a dress to go with them. I left him looking through his dress patterns and went home with a sense of impending doom.

Everyone's outfit was sorted now. The only thing I had to get was a pair of shoes and as my feet wouldn't even be seen under my dress I wasn't that bothered what shoes I wore. I was tempted to buy a pair with ankle straps just to upset my mother. If you've read my previous books you will know that my mother thought only prostitutes wore ankle strap shoes. This had caused a lot of confusion for me and Melanie when we were younger.

I happened to know now that this was complete rubbish. Now that I was going out into town drinking on a Saturday night I had passed some of the rougher pubs and I had seen actual prostitutes in action (well not actually in action but walking up and down looking for customers). I had made a point of looking at their shoes and not once had I seen any of them wearing ankle straps. Not that I could tell my mother this, if she thought I had seen 'ladies of the evening' she would have locked me in my room and never let me out again, not even for the wedding.

In the end, I bought a pair of plain cream sandals, they would do. It must seem strange to anyone reading this that I wasn't excited about my wedding or my dress or anything. It wasn't that I didn't want to get married, it was just that I wanted to get married my way. It really felt like this wedding was someone else's and I was one of the invited guests that really didn't want to go. It was just something that had to be got through so I could start my own life.

These days I spend more time planning my outfit to go to the shops than I did back then to get married. I hate my wedding photos and my stupid dress. I am often tempted to do my hair and make-up and go into a wedding shop, pick the nicest dress in there and get someone to take a picture. Finally, I would have a wedding photo that I liked, even if it was a bit late.

A few days later back at Frank and Sheila's the littlest bridesmaid's dress was almost finished. Frank had carefully looked at all the delicate colours on the pattern of the big dresses and decided the best colour to compliment them was bright orange. It was hideous. When I asked him where he had seen the colour orange on the other dresses he pointed to a tiny pale peach flower. I came to the conclusion he must be colour blind, this would explain a lot of Sheila's dresses and some of his shirts. I could only imagine the horror the poor little bridesmaid would be feeling when she saw it. She might have been only five but I well-remembered being five and being publicly humiliated by the clothes my mother used to dress me in.

I also came to the conclusion that it was a good job Frank hadn't met my mother first and married her. God knows what any offspring from those two would have looked like.

My mother was still pursuing her career as an Avon lady at this point. She had started selling the stuff a few years ago and kept getting in trouble with my dad for taking my brother with her on her rounds. She still took him whenever she couldn't get him to go to school (which was a lot) and my dad would go mad when he found out. My brother only put catalogues through letterboxes and then went around with my mother collecting them all back. It's not as if he was demonstrating the products or anything but that was still too much in my dad's eyes. It was for women, not boys and that was that. If anyone ever found out his son was an Avon lady he would never live it down.  My brother didn't care, he would have agreed to ballet dancing or flower arranging so long as it got him out of school.

My mother's career had never really taken off anyway. There was too much competition on the estate, every other house contained an Avon lady. She never made any money, just filled the house with 'overpriced pots of gunk' according to my dad.

She never even wore make up anyway, just a bit of lipstick and a touch of powder if she was going out. From time to time I would offer to 'do her up' and she would look really nice but she would complain that she couldn't stand the feeling of a heavy face (whatever that meant, I wasn't using cement) and she would wash it all off. She once agreed to let me 'tidy up' her eyebrows but that didn't go well.  I only plucked one hair and she let out a shriek that almost shattered the windows and ran out of the room calling me a 'bloody torturer'.  I told her you had to suffer to be beautiful but she said in that case she wouldn't bother, she'd managed this long, she'd stay as she was.

A couple of years before this I had my own eyebrows plucked for the first time. Me and my friend Tina had done each other's and we both got a bit carried away. The problem was getting them even, every time we took a bit off one side we had to do the other side to match. By the time mine were finished I had about three hairs left on each brow and I looked as if I was either really surprised or really quizzical. I knew when my mother came home from bingo she would have a fit.

She came in and headed for the kitchen, glancing at me, then she did a double take and her mouth fell open. She stood in front of me, a look of horror on her face and said

"What the hell have you done to your hair?"

So, on the whole, she was never really into make-up. I on the other hand had thrown myself whole heartedly into the world of cosmetics from the age of fourteen when I realized I could create myself a whole new face. I never went anywhere without the whole works on and even today I won't even put the bins out without my face on. My husband has strong feelings about my 'face' and he regularly tells people,

"I married a mask."

Nowadays bless him, he's so short sighted he can't tell if my face is on or off, I think he just sees a blur with a bit of yellow on top (I am also a natural blonde, number 9.3 in the

Nice and Easy range). It's a good job he's too scared to get his eyes lasered, he'd probably come home and wonder who the old lady in his living room was.

# CHAPTER SIX

## In the Box

It was the day the court case was due to begin and it was one of the hottest days we'd had that year. I had to turn up at work an hour early so that we had time to get to the next town and get to the right court in time. I was in a terrible mood before we even set off as I'd had to get up even earlier than usual and I was tired. Mr. Burton looked like he was in an even worse mood than me but Miss Turner looked like she was off for a nice day out. She was actually pleased with herself that she had got this case to court and someone was about to get what they deserved. You really didn't want to be on her hit list.

She took the front seat next to Mr. Burton and I was shoved into the back. I noticed she'd brought a packed lunch as if we were all off to the seaside, I hadn't even thought that far ahead and I didn't see Mr. Burton carrying any lunch boxes. I wasn't looking forward to the journey ahead.

It was very quiet all the way there, more than that it was a very uncomfortable silence. Mr. Burton smoked most of the way there, I think that was just because he knew Miss

Turner hated smoking. He kept doing his best to blow the smoke in her direction but most of it ended up going up my nose in the back. I couldn't blame him for taking it out on her but I wished the back windows would open.

When we arrived at the court we were shown into a waiting room. Apparently, we weren't allowed to sit in the same room as the poor shoplifter in case we intimidated him. Personally, I wanted to tell him I was sorry that he had to be put through all this just because of one self-righteous old biddy. I hoped he had someone to come with him for support.

We sat in that room nearly all day. It was boiling and boring and it was all I could do to stay awake. For the first hour, I tried to make polite chit chat and then I gave up and we all slipped into a coma. At lunch time Miss Turner opened her packed lunch and proceeded to stuff her face without offering us anything. Me and Mr. Burton went and found a cup of tea and bought a kit kat each from the sweet machine but, because it was so hot they'd all melted. He told me it was a perfect day for a round of golf and then shot an evil glance back at the room where Miss Turner sat, finishing her sandwiches and fruit.

Just when we'd resigned ourselves to sitting in that room all day someone came in and called for Miss Turner. She puffed herself up and left the room to go and ruin an old man's life. We waited for about half an hour and then a court official came in and said we could go and watch the proceedings from the public gallery if we were quiet so off we went.

It was all very grand, just like it was on the telly. I thought all these people must be sweating cobs under their wigs and gowns and hoped they'd put plenty of deodorant on that morning.

I heard Mr. Burton say,

"Good god, look at him." I turned to see what he was on about, he was looking at the poor old shoplifter in the dock. The poor old man we remembered from the shop now looked like a rich old man, he was wearing what seemed to be a really expensive suit, nothing like the ratty old coat he had hidden his swag in. His family were all there with him and they all looked very well to do. The woman we assumed to be his wife was dripping in gold.

The biggest change though was the bandage around his head and the crutches holding him up. He was playing the illness card. Apparently, he was so senile he didn't know what he was doing and since he had been arrested his condition had worsened and he had been having accidents.  He had brought his own lawyer to defend him.  I stopped feeling so sorry for him, I had thought the poor old bugger couldn't afford to buy food for himself. By the look of him now he could probably have bought the entire shop.

Miss Turner was in the witness box being interrogated by a tall man in a wig, she looked quite flustered and uncomfortable, good, I was glad about that. Then the man asked for exhibit B to be held up and some woman popped up holding the giant piece of toilet roll box that Miss Turner had written on. It was all too ridiculous. Me and Mr. Burton found this bit quite amusing.

Miss Turner was questioned for about half an hour but there was nothing she could say that was any different, she just kept telling the man the same thing over and over.  Eventually the judge woke up and told everyone to come back the next morning. I was well fed up then, I had been hoping all this would be settled on the first day. As well as that tomorrow was supposed to be my day off.

Miserably, we set off back for the car park.

None of us spoke much on the way home either. Miss Turner kept going on about how she'd been right to do what she did as the man was obviously a liar as well as a thief. Mr. Burton just grunted and resumed chain smoking and I got on with choking to death in the back. When we got back to the shop everyone wanted to know what had happened, was it exciting? I told them I'd had more fun watching my dad paint the toilet, then I went home to get ready to do it all again the next day.

When we arrived the next morning, we were shoved back in the same waiting room until after lunch. I couldn't imagine why it would take so long to decide if this man was guilty or not. It must have been costing a fortune for all this palaver and all for the sake of 95 pence.

After lunch (Miss Turner brought hard boiled eggs today), Mr. Burton was called in and me and Miss Turner sat in the gallery to watch. In the witness box Mr. Burton was having a hard time. The barrister or whatever he was called was accusing Mr. Burton of being a violent man with a vicious temper who had manhandled a poor pensioner. It was all nonsense, Mr. B was as mild mannered as my dad. The more he tried to explain himself, the more the barrister wound him up, trying to get him angry. I felt so sorry for him, he was being tied up in knots, he hadn't been prepared for this. I started to feel very nervous. I was up next and what would I be in for. I thought all I would have to do was identify a bit of cheese. Now I started to think I might be going down instead of the shoplifter.

In the box, Mr. B was starting to lose his temper exactly as the barrister intended. Just as he started raising his voice and getting a bit stroppy the barrister shouted,

"No more questions" and the judge sent us home until the next day again.

All the way home Mr. B was seething. I noticed he didn't smoke this time, he didn't need to, I swear there was smoke coming out of his ears. I was sitting in the back having a panic attack, I was dreading my turn the next day. Miss Turner was wittering on again about how she knew she was doing the right thing reporting this man, even if it did put us out a bit.

We had to drive home through some really quiet country lanes with no other traffic. I could see Mr. B in the rear-view mirror looking at all the hedgerows and I knew what he was thinking. If we killed Miss Turner and dumped her body behind one of those hedges it could be weeks before anyone found her.

When I got home that night and told my parents of the day's events they told me to be really careful the next day. No matter how nasty the barrister got with me, on no account was I to raise my voice or be cheeky. I should be polite and speak quietly and not do or say anything that might attract attention and get me in the papers. What did they think I was going to do?

The next day was even hotter, we set off for court early in the morning and it was already boiling. I was sick with nerves and Mr. B didn't look much better. He didn't know if they'd finished with him or if he was going to be dragged into the witness box and attacked again. I was cursing the day that silly old bugger came into our shop, and if he had to pinch something why did it have to be the one thing that I'd written on?

We had no sooner arrived at the court and been shoved into the waiting room again when a court official came and told us we were no longer needed. The case had been dropped and it was all over. All charges against the old man had been dropped and that was that, we were free to go. I was so relieved but Mr. B was fuming, we'd been dragged up and down for three days, he'd been publicly humiliated and all for nothing.

As we were talking, the old man and his family passed the door on their way out. He was stumbling along on his crutches, his family helping him. I felt like kicking one of his sticks out from under him. We said goodbye to the court man and made our way out to the car park. Mr. B said seeing as he'd already got someone in to cover for me I could take the rest of the day off. I noticed he didn't say the same thing to Miss Turner.

As we entered the car park we saw the old man and his family again. You can imagine how amused we were when we saw him throw his crutches into the boot of his big posh car and run around to open the door for his wife. As they drove away he waved to us and threw his bandage out of the window.

I thought Mr. B was going to have a fit, he was a very peculiar colour. He seemed to gather himself and then he turned to Miss Turner.

"Miss Turner, could I just say, the next time you see someone stealing from the shop, even if he's staggering past you holding the cash register, would you mind just KEEPING YOUR BLOODY MOUTH SHUT."

Her face was a picture, seeing that was almost worth the three days of my life that I would never get back.

# CHAPTER SEVEN

## And the List Goes On

The weeks seemed to be whizzing by now and the big day was looming ever closer. We realized we really should have sorted ourselves somewhere to live by now. We didn't want to leave it too late and end up having to stay with our families. Not that I would have had a choice anyway as my mother had done a deal with Joan next door and sold her my bed. I think she was all ready to swoop in and take it the minute I got my leg in the wedding car.

Joan was forever buying and swapping furniture with the neighbours. She had a very short attention span and soon got tired of her surroundings. Over the years, we had all got used to the sight of her husband Colin staggering up the road with sofas, wardrobes and wall units on his back. No sooner had he got things sorted than Joan would have a rethink and off he would go again, moving it all on to a different neighbour who fancied a change.

At one point, she amazed us all by actually swapping wallpaper with the woman who lived opposite us. Back then a new kind of wallpaper had just come out, you could peel this paper off in one long piece and it looked just the same as before you'd put it on. As all our houses were identical, she figured that both houses would have the same measurements and so they both just peeled off the paper, exchanged it, and then stuck it back up again in their own houses. It actually worked as well.

I used to feel sorry for Colin, as well as having a permanent stoop from carrying all the furniture, it must have been really confusing for him every night when he came home to a different house.

My mother never got involved with swapping stuff with Joan, my dad wouldn't allow it. He had a really big hang up about second hand things, if you couldn't afford new, you did without. He thought second hand things were beneath him, he didn't want other people's cast offs and if he ever caught us looking in second hand shop windows he would have a fit and drag us off down the road before anyone saw us.

It didn't matter if the things were only a week old, if they had belonged to someone else he didn't want any part of them. Because of this we missed out on a lot of bargains over the years, half of the stuff was better than what we had anyway. I never knew where this snobbiness had come from, he had grown up in the war when everyone had nothing and you made do and mended. Back in those days everyone pulled together in the community and shared whatever they had. My Nanna hadn't been like that and my Aunty Dolly was no snob, it was a mystery. Whenever I asked my mother why he was like that she would just say it was one of his little ways.

Sometimes he would allow my mother to take something Aunty Dolly didn't want any more but he was never happy about it and it didn't happen very often. So, my mother was banned from Joan's little swapping circle and had to make do with just being in the singing partnership with her.

For years now, ever since Joan moved in and burst into song in her kitchen they had been entertaining the neighbourhood. Before Joan my mother had put on solo concerts every teatime in the kitchen, causing half the kids in the street to wet their pants on a regular basis. Once Joan joined in the concerts took on a whole new direction and could be heard a lot further away as well. For a while a few years ago they had been joined by Lucky, our dog who liked to howl the backing track. If YouTube had been around back then they would have been an internet sensation.

I should have put a bit more thought into choosing the hymns for the wedding. I only knew the ones we'd sung at school so picked the two that I remembered liking the most. These were 'Oh Jesus I Have Promised' and 'He Who Would Valiant Be'. I never thought about it at the time but since hearing my mother practicing in the kitchen I had realized they both had really high notes in them.

I didn't care about reaching the high notes as I would be miming, the same as my dad. It was our usual routine at weddings and christenings. What worried me was the thought of my mother, strangling her vocal chords to hit the high notes. I knew from experience that it would be painful for the rest of the congregation. I hoped the vicar had the stained-glass windows well insured, there were sure to be a few cracks in them after she'd finished.

The invitations had all gone out now and after they'd all RSVP'd it looked like everyone would be turning up. For the last few weeks my mother had been ringing relatives she hadn't seen for years to tell them to expect an invitation. This was just an excuse to let them all know that I wasn't pregnant. Our real friends and close relations knew it wasn't a rushed affair as they knew we'd been engaged since last year.

My mother was worried that the rest of the family who we didn't see from one decade to the next would think that as I was so young there must be something fishy.

I told her to put it on the bottom of the invitations, next to the bit where she informed everyone that although my ring might look like silver, it was actually white gold and more expensive than yellow.

I found out that I wasn't too old to get a slap around the back of the head.

When all the replies were back I realized that I wouldn't know half the people at my wedding if I fell over them. They were all people who my parents and Frank and Sheila knew. I wouldn't recognize most of the people on my own wedding photos.

Two people I was happy to see were attending were my new grandparents. My nanna had died when I was eight and I had no memory of my grandads really so it was nice that I got some adopted ones. They were Frank's parents but they weren't like him at all. In fact, he thought they weren't good enough and hardly ever bothered with them even though they adored him. I wouldn't have been at all surprised to see him introducing some other elderly people as his parents at the wedding if he thought they looked a bit more in keeping. It's what he'd done for years with his kids.

We would go and visit Nanny and Grandad every Sunday afternoon and Nanny always made sure we had a Sunday dinner. It was thanks to Nanny that I discovered my love of swede. I had never had swede before, my mother only knew about peas and carrots and sometimes the odd sprout. When I first saw the orangey coloured pile on my plate I was a bit perplexed. When I tried it I loved it and ever since that day it has been my favourite vegetable. I have been known to eat just a plate of swede with gravy.

After I discovered it I tried to convince my mother to start cooking it. She said she didn't go in for all that 'foreign muck'. I told her it was grown here at home on British farms but she said I'd tried to tell her that about onions. We didn't eat spicy things in our house, when would I learn that?

Dear god, is there any wonder I never tasted curry until after I had left home. Frank and Sheila were just the same, I always thought Sheila and my mother must have been in the same cookery classes at school. Sheila was an appalling cook, whatever she cooked always came out looking completely different to how it should, even when you took the fag ash into consideration.

I have never cared for soup but, not long after I had been going round there she served up soup for our tea. I didn't know what kind it was but as I was slurping my way through it I announced to the table that this was the first time I had actually eaten soup. There was an uneasy silence before Sheila said quietly,

"It's stew".

Oops, apparently, my mother wasn't the only one who made unusual stew. Remember (if you have read my first book) hers was bright green. Anyway, it was nice to know we could always get a nice Sunday dinner at Nanny's house. Even if she did always lift my top up on the way out to see if I was wearing my vest.

Just as I was beginning to wonder if my nice new grandparents fancied a couple of lodgers, Frank and Sheila announced that one of their friends was working for a man who rented out houses all over the town. She was on the lookout for one for us and she had a couple in mind. This sounded quite exciting.

We really should have known better.

# CHAPTER EIGHT

## Jumping in With Both Feet

It was now half way through July and the wedding was only two months away. The weather was still hot and everyone was getting irritable with the heat, or maybe that was just in our houses. One Sunday me and my ever sooner to be husband went for a walk to get away from all the bickering. We must have been fed up as I have never known him walk anywhere since and I was all walked out from my early childhood rambling the East Coast with my parents.

We ended up a couple of miles away and decided to walk back alongside the river to see if it was any cooler, it wasn't. After we'd plodded along in silence for a bit (it was too hot to talk) I told him I couldn't go a step further without a sit down so we plonked ourselves down for a rest a few feet from the riverbank. I lay back for a spot of sunbathing and tried not to fall asleep. After a few minutes my intended decided it would be a good idea to go for a swim in the river, what better way to cool down? He has always been a good swimmer and is drawn to water like a seal, I on the other hand had only ever managed my five-yards breast stroke certificate at the school swimming baths and didn't really care for swimming that much. Admittedly if there had been a proper pool there I would have jumped in to cool down but nothing would make me put myself in the river. God knows what might be in there, lurking under the water, not to mention the odd shopping trolley or whatever other rubbish might have been dumped in there. Besides, I didn't have anything to put on for swimming.

I pointed this fact out to the Man from Atlantis but he said there was nobody to see him so he was going to go in naked and dry off in the sun. I told him he was mad but let him get on with it, I was too hot to argue and besides, he was right, there was nobody around for miles. I went back to my sunbathing, dimly aware that he was slinging clothes all over and thinking it was a good job my mother didn't know about this. If they thought I was marrying a nudist they'd have heart failure. What would the neighbours say about that one?

I heard,

Here I go then." as he thundered past me, heading for the edge of the water, then the next thing I heard was,

"Geronimo!" mingled in with an almighty scream and then a splash. What was he screaming about, and how could he make both noises at the same time?

He hadn't. What neither of us knew was that a few feet below us, further down the bank a lady had been sitting in the sun, quietly minding her own business and reading a book. She was obviously as unaware of us as we were of her. The first thing she knew of our presence was when a screaming, naked man flew over her, barely a foot above her head. God knows what she must have seen as he flew over the top of her, arms and legs akimbo. To add insult to injury he had soaked her as well when he landed in the water.

To be fair, he was mortified, so was she but she was nice about it when she eventually stopped hyperventilating. She averted her eyes as he climbed out of the water and ran for his clothes. It was a bit late for that really seeing as seconds before she had been almost nose to nose with his unmentionables but it seemed the polite thing to do.

While he got dressed I apologized again and assured her I would never let him out in public again without keeping a strict eye on him. It was to become a familiar speech over the coming years. He never meant for things to happen to him, he just had the same knack as me. Things always seemed to happen around us, maybe we were destined to find each other after all.

A few days later me and Vicky had the same day off from work so we went into town to do a bit of shopping. It was still boiling hot and dead uncomfortable. My hair was driving me nuts, my head was so hot I felt like I was wearing a hat. What I did next I can only blame on heatstroke. I walked straight into the nearest hairdressers and asked them to cut it all off. I showed the girl in the shop a picture in the book of a really short crop and said I wanted that.

Vicky kept trying to remind me that I had a wedding in two months and the photos would be there forever but I told her not to worry, it would be fine. After making sure that was really what I wanted (in front of witnesses) the girl got to work. When she had finished, it was really short but it didn't look much like the picture. Now that I had got some fresh air to my head reality started to sink in. What had I done? This was exactly the same thing my mother used to put me through, causing untold distress and I had gone and done it to myself.

Outside the shop I turned on Vicky, how could she let me go through with it? She was my bridesmaid, she was supposed to keep me out of trouble before the wedding. She said that was the Best Man's job, not hers and anyway, it might grow out a bit by then. I was thinking never mind the best man, when the groom saw the state of my head the wedding would probably be off anyway. What would he say?

Not a lot as it turned out. I think he was struck dumb that night when I opened the front door. Bless him, he did his best to hide it and even pretended he liked it but we both knew the truth. The only truthful thing he said was that now, on the wedding pictures he would have longer hair than me.

My mother loved it, which only served to prove what a terrible thing I'd done. She kept asking everyone,

"Doesn't she look like Doris Day?" As if that was going to make me feel any better. I felt like I was six years old again and she'd just done one of her hatchet jobs on me with the scissors

Frank and Sheila nearly had a duck fit when they saw it. Sheila said my hair was supposed to tumble down my shoulders over my wedding dress. I told her it already had, it tumbled all over my shoulders on its way to the hairdresser's floor. She wasn't amused.

Oh well, as Doris would say, Qey Sera Sera.

They didn't go on for too long though as they had some news for us. Their friend had found a small two bedroomed house for us to rent and she was letting us have it really cheap, although we were supposed to keep that bit to ourselves. She would meet us after work tomorrow with the keys. At last, a bit of good news, we were dead excited to go and have a look. A home of our very own with no nutty parents chipping in every five minutes, we couldn't wait.

The next night after I had finished work I got on the bus and went to have a look at my new house. We wanted to have a look on our own but Frank and Sheila had muscled in on the act again. The house was at the bottom of a small terrace, it had a big bay window and a small front garden, it seemed nice from the outside. Frank and Sheila's friend was waiting for us with the keys so we all piled in to have a look round. Inside it was nice as well, it had a big through lounge and a massive York stone fireplace (they were very 'in' back in the seventies). There was an extension built on the back that housed the kitchen and a downstairs bathroom. No back garden but a decent size yard with plenty of room for hanging out washing, we even had a shed. Upstairs were two bedrooms, a small one and a large front one over the bay window. It was all nicely decorated and didn't really need anything doing to it. Looking back, it was too good to be true.

We told the woman we definitely wanted it and she told us we had to pay a month's rent up front and sign a contract. We agreed to meet up again in a couple of days to finalize everything.

Two days later it was all sorted, we had a house. I had dragged my parents to see it and they liked it as well, my mother said it was a lot nicer than what they had started out with. All we needed now was furniture to fill it. We already had a few bits and bobs put away that we had bought and some things we had been given (much to my dad's disapproval), all we really needed were sofas and chairs, a bed and a washer.

When I was fifteen my parents had bought me a bedroom fitment, two double wardrobes with a dressing table and drawers in the middle. They said I could take this with me so we sorted a friend with a van to pick it up for us. This caused a bit of a fuss when we moved it and my mother spotted the big burn mark on the carpet that I had been hiding for the last two years. I had left my curling tongs on one day and they had fallen over and just about melted the carpet. I think practically every teenage girl in the seventies was hiding a burn mark on their bedroom carpet from curling tongs. Farah Fawcett had a lot to answer for.

My mother finally twigged why the wardrobes had been moved a few inches over from where they started and began going on about how sneaky it had been of me to hide it from her, why hadn't I told the truth, etc., etc. It had taken me most of a Saturday morning to shove them over the offending mark, they weighed a ton.

She didn't let me forget it for at least ten years, every time she saw me plug an appliance in she would pipe up,

"Be careful with that thing, it's hot, remember that bedroom carpet? I don't know where you learned to be so deceitful."

I did.

# CHAPTER NINE

## Let's Make Up

The big day was almost upon us, there were only a couple of weeks to go now. It felt like we were on death row waiting for the priest to read us the last rites, I was sure that wasn't how you were supposed to feel about your wedding day. People talked about it being the happiest day of your life but they'd told me that about schooldays as well and that was a big fat lie. We really wanted to be together, we just didn't want all the pandemonium that went with it.

Now that it was so close Frank and Sheila went into overdrive. They were laying down the law about everything. Looking back now we can't believe how we let them get away with it. My husband is so stubborn if you tell him to do anything he'll do the opposite just to be awkward and he has spent most of his life arguing with his family. There is absolutely no way anyone could ever call him a pushover but for some reason we just rolled over and let them walk all over us. I can only think it was because we just wanted to get it over with and get away from them.

They had taken over everything by now, even down to what fillings to have in the sandwiches. The most gob smacking thing we let them get away with though was the choice of best man. My (almost) husband naturally wanted his best friend who he had known since he was a kid. Frank and Sheila said no, he wasn't good enough, didn't look posh enough and wouldn't look good on the photos. They insisted he have his brother in law instead. This was his older sister Anne's husband and would prove to be awkward as by now Anne had told them how much she hated him and they had been separated for months.

We were all told that as far as anyone else was concerned, they were very happily married and would spend the day together, smiling, posing for photos, and acting as if they were the two most loved up people on the planet. On no account was anyone else at the wedding to find out what a failure she was at being a wife. It was unbelievable. Anne is also (apart from my husband) the most stubborn, assertive person I have ever met. They both tell it exactly as it is and don't take crap from anyone yet here they were, both of them going along with everything their parents wanted. I can only assume it was to do with their upbringing at the hands of these lunatics.

It made me grateful for my strange childhood. I was brought up by a pair of nutters but I always knew they loved me, well I knew my dad did. Even though he never told me, I always knew I was his little princess, even though thanks to my mother I looked more like the frog.

At least the pair of us would soon be away from all this madness and could get on with our new life without anyone interfering. I only had two weeks left and he had gone already, moving into the new house as soon as the bed was delivered. Frank and Sheila had sat him down for a last parental chat before he left them forever, telling him,

"If it doesn't work out, remember one thing. Don't ever come back here."

I thought that was quite sweet of them.

Back at my house the most important thing going on at the moment was my mother's search for a hat. It wasn't going well, she wasn't really a hat person, I don't know if it was because she was so short and round but nothing looked right. It didn't help that every hat she tried on was either met with a snigger from my dad or a roll of his eyes and a,

"Not likely, people will stare at us."

In the end, she settled on a small navy blue one that made her look like a girl guide leader or someone in the navy. Sheila, on the other hand had gone for the full 'Buckingham Palace Garden Party' look with a massive white floppy thing. It was awful but at least it hid most of her face so that was a bonus.

My dad, meantime was going through a crisis of his own. He had only just discovered that, as the father of the bride he would have to give a speech. This was his absolute worst nightmare, to stand up in front of a crowd and have them all look at him.

He demanded to know how long this had been going on. I told him as far as I knew it had been going on as long as people had been getting married. He said it was the first he'd heard of it, obviously forgetting the hundreds of weddings we had been forced to attend when I was young. And his own.

I don't think he slept much for those last few weeks after he found out, he was in complete terror.

The week before the actual wedding we all had to turn up for the rehearsal at the church. My parents left my little brother at home with Janice so that they could accompany me. We all arrived at the church at about the same time, I had my bridesmaids in tow but the little one wasn't there. It was agreed that on the day her mother would make sure she was where she was supposed to be.

For some reason that night I was having a bout of uncontrollable nervous laughter. It was agony trying to stifle it. I couldn't make eye contact with anyone for fear of losing control completely and wetting myself on the alter. I tried everything I could think of to hold it in, I bit my tongue until it bled, I thought of the saddest things I could, I dug my nails into my hands until I had holes in them, nothing helped. My dad noticed my red and quivering face and demanded that I stop it, right now. This only made matters worse.

My intended kept whispering in my ear, determined to find out what was so funny. I couldn't tell him as I didn't know but then he caught it as well and we were both holding it in. Behind me I could hear Vicky and Melanie tittering as well, apparently, I was infectious.

I could hear my mother asking my dad what was wrong with me but he didn't have a clue, anyway he was too terrified the vicar might ask him to give a run through of his speech. By the time the vicar got us to start practicing our vows we were so far gone we couldn't hold it any more. As soon as he started the 'Dearly beloved' speech we both burst out laughing and snorting, all the adults were appalled but looking at their disgusted faces just made us worse. Vicky and Melanie were holding each other up and crying with laughter. It seemed to go on forever, we couldn't get ourselves back under control. Eventually, after a few more snorts and a lot of hiccups I managed to apologies to the vicar and tell him it was just because I was so nervous. He said he quite understood, he saw it a lot (just not usually that extreme). He told us all to go on and get it all out of our systems so that it didn't happen on the actual day. He said he had another wedding booked in after us and he couldn't afford to run over while he waited for us to compose ourselves.

We pulled ourselves together and carried on with the rehearsal, it was quite simple really. All we had to do was turn up and repeat whatever the vicar told us, I thought even we could manage to do that.

Outside the church, we all got a telling off from both sets of parents for showing them up but we didn't care. Somehow, I didn't think we would be spending much time laughing on the actual day.

We all went back to Frank and Sheila's for a cup of tea (still not P.G Tips) as they lived not far from the church. Cheryl and Alistair were there but gave us a frosty reception and left the room more or less straight away. They were still annoyed at us for something that had happened the week before and they were holding a grudge. It was quite funny really, well we thought so.

We had all been on a works outing to Blackpool to see the lights. Our two best couple friends, Gary and Sarah were with us, they had already been married for a year. Cheryl and Alistair were there as well as all the lads worked at the same place. It had been a good day but a long one and we were all glad to get back on the coach and head for home. I was clutching a giant teddy bear and trying to find a spare seat to put it in. I had seen all these girls carrying them around the fair, their boyfriends had won them for them. Me and Sarah at once instructed our other halves to win one for us. It wasn't as easy as we thought, the stalls were obviously rigged and they wasted loads of money attempting to beat each other at various tasks and win a teddy in the process.

After about an hour of this, Gary told Sarah that she could bloody do without one, they had nowhere to put a stupid giant stuffed bear anyway, and my other half did a deal with the man on the stall and bought one for a few quid. It worked out a lot cheaper. I think this was how most of the girls I'd seen carrying them had acquired theirs as well.

We hadn't seen Cheryl and Alistair all day, they had gone off on their own. They always went off on their own, calling each other silly names and acting dead soppy. It was sweet for a bit but after a while it was so sweet it made you want to throw up.

They were nearly the last two on the coach and turned up wearing matching 'Kiss Me Quick' hats and clutching bags full of sticks of rock and giant humbugs. We all got settled and the coach set off for home.

The first hour was quite uneventful until a couple further down the coach started arguing. It started with just the odd comment and quickly escalated into a full scale nuclear meltdown. I think they had spent most of the day in the pubs and that wasn't helping. When one of them started slamming the other one's head into the window the driver decided enough was enough. He stopped the coach and told them to pack it in or he would throw them off the bus. Then he told the rest of us to keep an eye on them. If he had to stop the bus again he would throw us all off and drive away. This was just like being back at school on the annual school trip.

Before he could get started again the woman stood up, gathered her stuff together and told him she was getting off anyway, there was no way she was spending another minute with this pig. With that she got off. The driver tried to stop her, we were in the middle of nowhere and it was dark out there. She told him in no uncertain terms to mind his own business and got off anyway.

We were all looking at her husband, surely, he wouldn't leave her out there on her own? Anything might happen to her. He just shrugged his shoulders and told the driver to get a move on, so he did. The last we saw of her she was staggering along in the dark with a load of bags and a giant stuffed orangutan.

After we had all got over that we settled back down for the rest of the journey. After a while we noticed Cheryl and Alistair were fast asleep. As I had my make-up bag with me we thought it might be fun to give Alistair a make-over, we thought it might give him a nice surprise when he woke up. All I can say is he was a heavy sleeper. Half the bus got involved, adding on bits here and there until he looked like Dolly Parton in a coma. Cheryl was still snoring on beside him with no clue what we were up to.

When we couldn't possibly get any more make up on his face we settled back in our seats and waited for them to wake up. It took a while. When we got fed up of waiting one of the lads sitting behind them kicked the back of their seats. They both awoke at the same time. Cheryl turned to smile at Alistair and got the shock of her life when she saw Danny la Rue sitting next to her. She let out a blood curdling scream which sent Alistair into a blind panic as he didn't know what she was screaming about and he started shrieking as well.

The whole bus was in hysterics, even the driver was crying with laughter, which was a bit worrying as we were hurtling down the motorway at the time. Cheryl went nuts, demanding to know who had done this thing, she wanted to know why we hadn't stopped it, we were family. Stopped it? We were the ones who had started it. To make matters worse there was no way for poor Alistair to wash it off on the bus. Everyone donated tissues but he had so much gunk on his face all he could do was spread it all around. Cheryl tried to help out by spitting on his hanky but eventually she ran out of spit and he had to get off the bus at the other end looking like a clown that had been involved in a nasty accident.

They both said they would never speak to us again and we could stuff our wedding, they weren't going to come. I knew they would, there was no way Frank would let them miss it. I just hoped they could get all the make-up off by then.

It could have been much worse, luckily no one had brought a camera. If we all had camera phones and Facebook like we do today the pictures would have been around longer than the two of them.

Anyway, it was a week later now and they still weren't seeing the funny side. Admittedly, Alistair was still going to work every day with black rings around his eyes, it was taking a while to get it all off properly. He looked a bit like a faded Alice Cooper.

All in all, it had been an eventful day, those two were more in love than ever, taking the rest of the world on together while the other two from the bus were getting a divorce. Blackpool had a lot to answer for.

Cheryl's last word, before she stopped talking to us completely was that we would never last, we were too childish to be married people. I filed it away with every other bit of marriage advice I had been given.

The best piece of advice about marriage I had been given was from my new nanny a few weeks before. She told me the secret to a long and happy marriage was to never go to bed angry. She said that was why she and grandad had been married for fifty years. Maybe that's why we've lasted so long, we have always followed nanny's advice, we never, ever go to bed angry. We stay up and fight.

# CHAPTER TEN

## Time to Grow Up

It was the day before the wedding and my last day at work as a single woman. All day the customers were coming in to give me their best wishes, some even brought me cards. It was dead nice of them to bother. Mr. B had printed me a new name badge with my new name on it. That would take some getting used to, I had been practicing calling myself by my new name but it sounded strange. I knew for the first few weeks if anyone ever called me by it I would probably ignore them, not realizing that was me.

My workmates couldn't all come to the actual wedding as they were needed there all day. The two older ladies, Jill and Yvonne didn't work weekends so they were coming with their husbands and everyone else was coming to the night time 'do'. We were having this at a club just around the corner from our new house, we had booked the function room and hired a mobile disco. Mr. B said he wasn't going to come as it would be too weird for me to have my boss there, I think it was really because he didn't like his wife much and also, he was scared we dropped him in it about how much time he spent playing golf. We always said he was in a meeting if she rang the shop while he was out.

Miss Turner hadn't mentioned the wedding since the day after my engagement party when she had called me a silly girl. I never invited her as it would only be giving her the chance to throw a bit more abuse at me. For a Christian lady, she was a very unpleasant person.

After lunch Mr. B called me into the back of the shop, he asked me if I'd forgotten anything about the wedding. I did a mental check, flowers, cars, photos, guests, all sorted. It was more Frank and Sheila's list than mine anyway. I said no, I didn't think so, it was all organised. He said he had one thing he knew I'd forgotten, I started to panic, what could it be, I had no time to sort it out, whatever it was.

Then he pointed to the works rota on the wall where we always booked our days off if we needed to swap with someone. There was my name all penned in to work the next day, I'd completely forgotten to ask for the day off. Mr. B pulled a dead serious face and said there was no way he could spare me tomorrow, we would be too busy with it being a Saturday. I almost had a heart attack, how could I tell my mother about this?

Then he started laughing and said he was only joking, he had sorted everything out a few weeks ago, he was just waiting to see if I would remember. For a few seconds, I thought this might be a way out for us, we could get out of everything and have our wedding later the way we wanted. The thought didn't last long though. If I told our parents that after all the trouble they'd gone to, I would probably have to leave the country.

Mr. B said it was a good job Mr. Streep, the area manager hadn't got wind of my forgetfulness. He would have made me come into work in my dress and just let me out for an hour for the ceremony if I begged hard enough. He was right, Mr. Streep was horrible, we all called him Creepy Streepy. He didn't walk, he slithered, before you even knew he was in the shop he was behind you, breathing down your neck. He was so slimy he practically dripped as he slithered along.

He used to pop (slither) in a couple of times a week to check up on us. He didn't like our shop, he thought we let the side down. Because we were such a small shop our sales figures could never match up to the bigger stores around the region, he thought we should put more of an effort into selling stuff. I don't know how he thought we should go about this, having Miss Turner walking up and down the street wearing a sandwich board always came to mind but nobody would ever dare mention that, even as a joke.

He hadn't been at all amused about the shoplifting saga, he said if it had got into the papers it would have been bad publicity (he was just like my parents on that one). Whenever we made a mistake in the running of the place and tried to cover it up he always found out about it. Thank god he never found out about the time I over-ordered the piccalilli and ended up ordering 240 jars instead of 24, we managed to keep that from him. Because we hardly ever sold any piccalilli, Wayne helped me hide it all over the warehouse, it was stashed away all over the place for years.

Wayne was dead funny, he was only sixteen and this was his first job. Even though me and the other girls were only a year older than him we treat him like our baby brother and looked after him. His mother had died when he was young and he did all the housework and looked after his little sister as well as working a full-time job. Despite this, I never saw him without a smile on his little face and we all loved him.

Every tea break he would entertain us by telling us the plot of the latest film he'd just seen or sing us the latest song he'd just bought. The album 'War of the Worlds' had just been released and Wayne was one of the first to buy it. For weeks, we heard nothing else from him, he spent every tea break explaining the plot and every day he would entertain us with another song from the album. I can never hear a song from that album without picturing Wayne in the tea room, almost spilling his tea with excitement as he sang us his latest song.

A couple of months before, we had all narrowly missed getting sacked because of Wayne's antics. It was a Tuesday and it was Miss Turner's day off. Because it was a nice day, Mr. B decided a nice round of golf was called for. It wasn't one of Creepy Streepy's days for popping in, he did the bigger shops on a Tuesday, so Mr. B took off for a couple of hours, leaving us in charge.

Looking back, he was asking for trouble. We were like naughty schoolkids whenever we were left in charge without Miss Turner or Mr. B. We used the telephone for personal calls, took tea breaks willy-nilly whenever we felt like it and ate as many chocolate biscuits from the shelves as we felt like.

About an hour after Mr. B left the shop the phone rang, it was Creepy Streepy wanting to speak to Mr. B. Debbie answered the phone and told him Mr. B had just popped out for a minute. He asked to speak to Miss Turner but Debbie told him it was her day off. He said he would call back later that afternoon. That would be ok, Mr. B would be back by then.

A bit later on Wayne was filling the freezer in the back as we had just had a frozen food delivery. As we were such a small shop we only had one freezer, a big chest one that doubled as my cheese cutting area once a week. Wayne had just finished throwing in the last few bags of frozen peas and fish fingers. I think he was feeling a bit giddy with the excitement of having no bosses there to order him around as, out of the blue he decided to see if he could fit me in there as well.

He was a lanky lad, a lot taller than me but I never realized he was so strong, in my defense though I never saw it coming. He picked me up in a flash and pretended to drop me in the freezer, I was kicking and protesting so much he lost his grip and I fell into the freezer with just my legs sticking out. Debbie was screaming with laughter watching me fighting to get out among all the chips and fish fingers and Wayne was apologizing saying he was only joking and hadn't meant me to fall in. He was just about to pull me out when Kim, the other girl ran in and shouted that Creepy

Streepy was in the shop and heading straight for us.

There was no time to get me out, we were all in for it now. Before I knew what was happening, Wayne shoved my legs into the freezer and hissed, "Stay down", before closing the lid on me. He left it open a couple of inches so that I could see out but I was horrified, I have always been claustrophobic, this was my worst nightmare.

Seconds later Creepy Streepy entered. Debbie, Wayne and Kim all stood in front of the freezer, hoping he wouldn't notice that it was open a bit. I daren't move in case he heard the frozen peas creaking underneath me. He asked where Mr. B was. Debbie gave him the same speech about how he had just popped out for a minute.

"You said that over an hour ago" said Creepy. Debbie told him he had come back just after that phone call but now he had just popped out again. It was obvious Creepy didn't believe her, he sensed something was up. Then Debbie had a brainwave and asked him to come and give his opinion on something she'd just moved around on the shelves. Ever the busybody he followed her out into the shop, leaving the other two to help me escape my frozen box.

I could have killed Wayne but one look at his white face changed my mind, he was frightened to death. If he'd got us all sacked he would never have been able to forgive himself, plus he really needed this job to help out at home. We'd got away with it this time but we never messed about that much again whenever we were left on our own and we always kept an eye out for Creepy. That was the only time Wayne's daft grin ever slipped.

Just a few months ago I drove past the shop, I don't live in that area these days so I didn't think the shop would even be there anymore. To my amazement it was still there, it didn't even look that different to when I was last there. The warehouse doors were painted a different colour and the trolleys outside were a lot newer but that was about all.

I felt all nostalgic as I drove up the road, I wondered if there were still any jars of piccalilli hidden away, still gathering dust at the back of the shelves in the warehouse.

Just before I left for home on my last ever day as a 'Miss', Mr. B went into the cupboard and brought out a big wedding present, all wrapped up. Everyone had chipped in to buy it for us, there was a big card as well, signed by everyone, even Miss Turner. I was really touched, I had no idea they'd been planning anything. They all wished me well, the ones who would be coming said they would see me tomorrow and that was it. I was going home for the last time to get ready for my wedding.

Even after all the months of planning, now that it was here I couldn't quite believe it. I wondered how the next day would turn out. How would I be feeling this time tomorrow?

# CHAPTER ELEVEN

## No Going Back Now

It was here, the day everyone had been planning for since last Christmas. I woke up feeling sick with nerves and went downstairs for my last ever family breakfast in this house. Downstairs my mother was in a panic.

"It's about time you were up, I was just going to shout you" she said, "you need to start getting ready soon".

It was only eight o clock and the wedding wasn't until one. I told her it wouldn't take me five hours to put on my dress and my face. I was a lot younger in those days and my face didn't need all that much time, nowadays it's a much bigger job and takes a lot longer.

She told me to eat as much as I could, it would be a long day and I would need to keep my strength up. I told her I was getting married not entering a triathlon but she didn't laugh, she was too stressed. She was having second thoughts about her hat, she said but it was too late to do anything about it. Luckily, she had found the perfect shoes and matching handbag. My dad was ironing his best shirt as he made a much better job of ironing things than my mother did, he looked like he hadn't slept and I knew he was a lot more nervous about today than I was. I told him not to worry about his speech, all he really had to do was thank people for coming, I wasn't expecting him to go rambling on for ages. He just seemed to become more engrossed in his ironing and I realized he was doing his old trick of pretending it wasn't happening, he was shoving it out of his mind until he was forced to deal with it. This was how he had lived his whole life.

I tried to eat a bit of toast with my cup of tea and went up to have a bath. Vicky and Melanie wouldn't be coming until about eleven o clock, the cars were booked for quarter past twelve, giving us plenty of time to get to the church.

After my bath, I rang Frank and Sheila's house to see what state the groom was in, he had stayed there the night before so they could make sure he got to the church before I made my big entrance. I asked him how he was feeling.

"Sick", was the reply.

"Me too" I said, "do you think that's normal?"

"Probably, especially with our families."

"Ok then, see you in a bit"

"Ok".

You would have thought we were just off to the pictures, not to our wedding. I think we would have been happier with that, watch a film then nip in the registry office on the way home and get hitched. Back home in time for tea and a few drinks down the pub with our mates. That would have been our perfect wedding. Just us and nobody fussing or interfering.

It was far too late for that now, like it or not, this was going to be a big wedding.

My mother said people would remember this one. I told her that's what I was afraid of.

I went back upstairs to what was left of my bedroom. The only thing left in there now was my bed and a couple of boxes of bits and bobs, everything else had already been taken to the new house. Everything was organised down there now, all ready for us to move into later. I started to put my make up on and do something with my hair, what was left of it. It had grown out enough now so that I could get the tongs on it but it was still short. Oh, if I had known about all the hair extensions of the future, I could have been gliding down the aisle trailing my hair behind me if only I had a time machine.

I didn't, so I did the best I could with what I had. My mother banged on the door on her way to the bathroom.

"You be careful with them bloody curling tongs, I don't want another burn mark on my carpet."

She had been perfectly content for the last two years, not knowing about the burn. All she had to do was put a rug over it anyway. That's what my family did best anyway, sweep everything under the rug and never speak of it again. Once she'd covered it up it would simply cease to exist anymore. Like most of my childhood.

At eleven o clock my bridesmaids arrived and I got a bit excited, they were so enthusiastic I got swept along with them. They helped me sort the veil and head dress out without making any more of a mess of my hair, then I helped them to pin their hats on. It was a nice sunny day outside but it was windy, I didn't want them to be running around outside when the photos were being taken, trying to catch their hats. The little bridesmaid was going to meet us at the church, her parents were bringing her.

Eventually, we were all ready. I had my stupid dress on, I still didn't like it but everyone else said it looked lovely. You have to say that to a bride don't you, nobody is ever going to say,

"Is that what you're wearing?"

Little did I know that in a couple more years, Lady Diana Spencer would walk down the aisle to marry Prince Charles, wearing a crumpled old thing that looked like a giant dishrag. At least my dress was nicer than that and I bet hers cost more than £30 from Debenhams.

Even my mother said I looked lovely, my dad went a bit red and said,

"About time you wore a frock", while my brother just giggled as if it was dead funny.

At least I looked better than he did, he had refused all the clothes my mother had tried to buy him. She wanted him to wear a nice pair of trousers and a smart blazer. In the end they compromised, he agreed to the trousers but wore his anorak with them, the only thing that made him look any different was the pink carnation my mother pinned to it.

My dad had his new suit on, it was exactly the same as his old one but then, he never liked change. My mother was in a navy-blue coat that matched her hat and made her look even more like a girl guide leader. She had her new matching white shoes and handbag as well (she didn't usually wear odd shoes, I mean they matched the handbag), and she was also wearing a small carnation on her coat.

Before we knew where we were it was time to go. The first car was for my mother, brother and the bridesmaids, me and my dad would follow on in the bridal car. We all made sure we had the right flowers. Terence had made us all silk arrangements so we could keep them he said, Vicky and Melanie had peach and white posies while I had red roses with little white flowers scattered among them.

We all went outside where the neighbours were waiting to shout congratulations (and have a good nosey). Joan was on the doorstep and followed us to the cars to wave us off, I wondered if my mother had left her a key so that she could get my bed out.

I had to hand it to Frank and Sheila, the cars were lovely, big long white ones decorated with ribbons and flowers. Even my parents couldn't find fault with them. My mother and brother got into theirs with Vicky and Melanie and me and my dad got into the other one. As we moved off down the street the neighbours were all waving while the little kids from the street ran behind us until they couldn't keep up.

I had always thought that when the bride to be was in the car with her father he would have a final talk with her and make sure she really wanted to go through with the wedding. I had imagined him telling her if she had changed her mind it wasn't too late to call it off and he wouldn't think any less of her. In this car, those roles were reversed.

My dad was so nervous I thought he might throw up, I think if I had offered to turn the car around and call the whole thing off he would have gone along with it without a second thought.

It was an awkward journey, he tried to make small talk for a while and then ended up making fun of my mother's hat while making faces at my brother in the other car. I wondered what the driver was making of it all, I expect he had seen all sorts before.

It took about half an hour to get to the church, it was in a little village not far from the estate where Frank and Sheila lived. There was nothing there really except a few houses, the church, a little shop and a couple of farms. When we pulled up outside there were a few people milling around but most of them were already inside. I spotted my little bridesmaid before the car even stopped. To be fair you couldn't really miss her in her fluorescent orange dress. By the look on her face I don't think her mother was too impressed with

Frank's handiwork. I looked around at the faces of the other people but didn't know most of them from Adam. Frank and Sheila came rushing over as we got out of the car to tell us all how lovely we looked. This was the moment my mother and Sheila realized that they had bought identical shoes and handbags. They would look like a pair of book ends on the photos. As soon as I got out of the car the wind caught my veil and blew it straight up over my head. I hoped there would be a sheltered spot where we could take the photos otherwise it would be an interesting wedding album. Vicky and Melanie were already holding onto their hats in case the pins weren't enough.

The church bells were ringing which I hadn't been expecting. Frank said he'd paid extra for that, he was acting as if he'd paid for everything when in fact we had all shared the cost. I asked about my groom, they said he was inside, waiting with his best man (the one he didn't like and barely spoke two words to when he was married to his sister). She was outside as well, looking so miserable I felt sorry for her. She hadn't spoken to her husband since they had split up and now she was having to play happy families with him for the full day.

Cheryl and Alistair were also outside, they had forgiven us now for the bus incident and we were all friends again (I thought). The vicar was waiting outside with everyone else, he said hello to my parents again and told us we would be starting in a few minutes. He said he would give us a little while to get inside and get ourselves organised and when he got the signal from the church warden he would tell the organist to start the music. That would be our cue to start walking down the aisle, he reminded us what we'd been shown at the rehearsal. Slow, careful steps, taking our time so that the organ player could get all the music out. Also, to give everyone a chance to have a look at us as we walked past them. This was the worst thing he could have told my dad, he didn't want to be looked at. I told him it would be me and my dress they would be looking at, no one ever looked at the bride's father. I don't think I convinced him.

Everyone except me and my dad and the bridesmaids went inside to take their seats and we went into the little porch to get sorted out. Vicky adjusted my veil for me and then we took our places. Me and my dad in front, followed by the little bridesmaid and the other two bringing up the rear. Me and the bridesmaids had all practiced keeping in step and we had got it all sussed. I just had to try and keep my dad at the same pace as the rest of us.

When we were all ready, the church warden went off to tell the vicar. A minute later the first bars of the Wedding March filled the air. I took a deep breath, we all wished each other luck and we were off. This was it. When I walked back outside I would be walking out as a married grown up woman.

# CHAPTER TWELVE

## A Carry-On Wedding

We started to take our first few steps down the aisle. The church was packed with people, I was shocked how many had actually turned up. At the first sound of the organ all the heads turned in our direction. I was supposed to take my dad's arm as we'd rehearsed but before I had time to do that he started to panic. When the first few bars of the Wedding March finished and the actual music began, it had the same effect on my dad as a starting pistol. He grabbed my elbow and took off up at the aisle at an alarming rate. The expectant, smiling faces turned into one big blur as we sped past them, the bridesmaids were practically running behind us trying to keep up. I was worried the little one would get trampled. I released my elbow, linked arms with him and tried my best to hold him back a bit but it was no use. My dad was on a mission to get me to the vicar as quickly as humanly possible. His eyes were fixed on the alter like Linford Christie must have looked at the finishing line, he had a goal and he was going for it.

We reached the alter before the organist had even really got started. As she had her back to us she didn't know we were already there so she kept on playing. In her head, we were still at the back of the church, making our way along slowly and gracefully. The vicar didn't seem to know what to do, he couldn't really shout,

"Oi, Doris, you can stop now" so she kept on playing. We were all standing there awkwardly, the bridesmaids were trying to catch their breath and I was saying hello to the groom who was looking decidedly shell shocked. He hadn't been expecting me to arrive that fast. He told me I looked lovely, we had time for quite a chat before someone went up and told Doris (I don't think that was really her name) that she could have a breather.

The music stopped abruptly and the service began. We had the 'Dearly Beloved' bit and I was relieved to find out I wasn't about to have a fit of the nervous giggles again. It's a good job everyone was behind me so I couldn't see the confusion on their faces, that might have set me off. The vicar waffled on for a bit and then we all sang the first hymn that we'd picked, I think all of us at the alter were miming or maybe we were just drowned out by my mother. I had been right about the high notes, I swear at one point the vicar was wincing.

When we'd finished, the vicar asked who was giving this woman away, instantly my dad gave me a shove towards the groom and ran to sit down next to my mother. We were asked to kneel down in prayer, which created the first scene of the service. I was half way down when I got the heel of my shoe caught in my dress. I don't even know how it happened but I was stuck half way between kneeling and standing. I must only have been stuck for a few moments but it felt like an eternity as I bobbed up and down in a demented curtsy.

After a few more bobs, my nearly husband heaved me back upright while I got my foot free, then we knelt down properly. The vicar took a scarf from around his neck and tied our hands together. I wasn't expecting that, he had made no mention of this in the rehearsal. At the same time, I noticed that my groom seemed to have developed a really bad tremor, his hands were shaking so badly that my hand, tied to his joined in.

"What's the matter" I whispered.

"Don't know, can't stop shaking" he whispered back through chattering teeth. I had figured that already.

After a bit more waffling, the vicar untied us and asked who had the ring. The best man that nobody liked popped up and handed it to the vicar who hissed "Not to me, to him". He gave it to my groom who got ready to put it on my finger. We did the whole 'With this ring I thee wed' thing then he went to place it on my finger which is where it went a bit wrong again.

I don't know if it was nerves but my fingers seemed to have swelled up. The ring which a week before had fitted me perfectly now wouldn't even go past my knuckle. After a bit of shoving and me whispering 'Ow' the vicar stepped in again.

"Spit on it dear" he whispered.

What, in church? That didn't seem very dignified. I tried to discreetly lick my finger and with a bit more shoving it went on. When it was on we said a few more words and that was it, the vicar pronounced us man and wife, we had done it.

Before we could leave we had to sing another hymn. Once again, I could hear my mother above everyone else. I realized this was the first time Frank and Sheila had heard her singing voice, I could only imagine what they were thinking. When we had finished pretending to sing it was time to walk back up the aisle together. This time we went a bit slower and I got to spot a few faces in the crowd who I knew.

Aunty Dolly was at the front, waving to us, Uncle Malcom and Janice and Malcom Jnr were with her. I spotted a couple of friends but everyone else I looked at I didn't recognize, they were all smiling though so I smiled back. Frank's brother Gerry had already run outside to be ready with his camera when we came out of the doors.

We stepped outside for our first look at the outside world as man and wife. Instantly I was hit in the face by a ton of confetti thrown by Cheryl, that made me think maybe she wasn't quite as over our tiff as she said she was, it could have been worse though, she could have left it in the box.

People were filing out of the church behind us, everyone wishing us good luck and congratulations. Gerry wanted everyone out of the way so he could start playing with his camera. He got everyone to wait out of the way while he started snapping away, it took forever. We had a few taken on our own, then he brought in family of the bride, then family of the groom, then friends of the bride, friends of the groom, these were mostly the same people because they were my friends and his friends (we were very friendly). On and on it went, people being maneuvered around all over the place. Every time my mother got into a photo with us she kept shoving my flowers to one side. When I asked her what she was doing she said it was to show everyone I wasn't hiding any little secret behind my bouquet. She was still worried all the distant relatives would think I was pregnant. I should have got the vicar to make an announcement. At one point, even he was in the photos as well.

When Gerry had nearly finished, he took a photo of everyone that was there, he had to stand so far back for to get everyone in he was practically in the next field. Everyone was squashed in and you can hardly tell who's who they all look so small. It's a good job my dad never took the photo, everyone would have been pointing at the vicar. (If you haven't read the last book you won't get that bit).

After the photos were finished it was time for the reception, the village hall had been hired for the occasion as it was only a short walk from the church. To get to it all the guests walked across the old cemetery which had been there for hundreds of years while we got to ride about twenty yards in the wedding car, no walking for us.

This was where it went a bit wrong again. Because it was such a small village and hardly anyone lived there, the cows from the nearby farm were free to roam about wherever they pleased. Apparently, it pleased them a lot to roam through the cemetery, leaving little presents for everyone. I'm lying here, they weren't little, they were massive, and sloppy and recent.

My mother was first to notice this and immediately appointed herself as chief cowpat spotter. She barged in front of everyone shouting,

"Excuse me ladies and gentlemen, watch out for the cowpats." I really believe that had never been said at a wedding before that day. She was so busy trying to look important and charging around making sure everyone had got the message that she didn't look where she was going and landed ankle deep in a massive steaming one.

She was mortified, so was my dad who immediately disowned her and went off in front with my brother. Frank and Sheila were laughing like drains, Sheila said it should have happened before the photos, at least then their shoes would have been different colours.

We arrived at the village hall which had been decked out with big tables and lots of chairs. The cake had pride of place at its own special table. It was beautiful, the cake lady had done us proud, I was glad to find out later that Gerry had taken photos of it before it was ruined forever. Another table had been set aside for everyone to put the wedding presents on and there was quite a pile already. My mother ran off to get cleaned up as some of the guests were gagging and we took our place by the door to greet everyone as they came in.

One by one they filed past, I lost count of how many people said to me,

"The last time I saw you, you were only this big" pointing to their knees. I never realized I had been so short. My mother's older sister came along after a while, she was the one who everyone had always talked about, the one who kept all the American soldiers entertained during the war. I hadn't seen her for years but noticed she still had the same bright orange face, she was almost the same colour as the little bridesmaid's dress. Big sister Anne grabbed us both in a big hug and said,

"I hope you'll be as happy as I am" with tears in her eyes, then she added "Now that I've left the bastard."

After what seemed hours, they had all been seated and we could finally grab a seat ourselves. We were on a big long table with both families, the best man that nobody liked and the bridesmaids. Terence's still oblivious wife Marjorie had put on a buffet so everyone could mingle. She hadn't outdone herself. She had gone with endless amounts of sausage rolls, ham sandwiches, crisps and sausages, cheese and pineapple on sticks. It was typical seventies party food.

We got ourselves settled, had a glass of wine and suddenly Frank dug my new husband in the ribs and told him it was time for his speech. He wasn't looking forward to it any more than my dad was but he gave it a go. He did the 'My wife and I' thing and everyone laughed and applauded, then he thanked everyone for coming, thanked the bridesmaids, thanked everyone who had got everything ready, then sat down and ordered a pint.

Meanwhile my dad decided this was the time to go for his big moment. He jumped up from his seat, shouted,

"Thank you all for coming" then sat down again before anyone realized he had actually stood up at all. The relief on his face was obvious even to a blind man.

Half an hour later everyone was getting stuck into the food and drink and people were starting to mix as both families started introducing each other. Gerry, meanwhile was going around the room taking 'candid' shots of everyone. Seeing the results afterwards, they seemed to consist of pictures of people mid conversation, mouths hanging open, eyes all over the place or, even worse, people eating, shoving large amounts of food down their throats. It wasn't attractive.

We didn't have any music, I don't know if that had been overlooked or if it was because we were having the disco later. Either way, my little brother proved to be the entertainment for the afternoon. He decided that, being just nine years old now it was a good time for him to start drinking. He had been paired up at the reception with the little bridesmaid's older brother who was the same age as him.  I don't know who started it but they began going table to table, finishing off every glass of beer they came across, my parents obviously weren't keeping their usual eye on him.

My brother turned into the life and soul of the party, far from being the nervous, jumpy, shy boy that he usually was in company, he went around the room introducing himself to everyone, telling jokes (well, trying), and spouting all kinds of nonsense to anyone who would listen. He is still the same now when he's had a few. It was hysterical.

After the buffet had been reduced to a few crumbs and most of the drink had been polished off (a lot of it by my brother), it was time to cut the cake. We had to make a big show of this for some more photos. When we had finished, the cake was whisked away from under our noses to be cut into pieces for everyone. They descended on it like locusts, everyone got a piece and then pretended they hadn't had any so needed to take a piece home. The next time I saw it there was nothing left but the ornament off the top and a couple of fruit crumbs. They had demolished it. I had heard of an old wives' tale about sleeping with a piece of wedding cake under your pillow. It's a good job I didn't want to try this, whatever was supposed to happen probably wouldn't be the same if all you had to sleep on was a currant.

After the cake had been distributed things were winding down and people were taking their leave, some of them said they would see us later. The ones who had only come for the free food and drink would probably die before we ever saw them again.

My parents ordered a taxi to take my brother home. He was carried out fireman style over my dad's shoulder singing 'Gone fishin'' at the top of his lungs. I was only finding out now what a little comedian I had been living with all these years.

Eventually there was only me and my new family and the best man that nobody liked left. Now that everyone had gone he and Anne could stop pretending and go back to hating each other. It was an awful day for her, having to stick to his side all day. All the relatives and friends that hadn't seen them for ages kept asking when they were going to hear the 'pitter patter of tiny feet'. The only sound of feet they were likely to hear were hers, pitter pattering all over his head.

At last all the presents had been rounded up and put in Terence's car, he was taking them back to Frank and Sheila's for now along with us two. We were going to get changed there and then go home to our new house to get ready for the night time disco.

We were exhausted already. I was dreading having to go through it all again later. At least all our proper friends would be there for that. We climbed in the car and set off, unaware that in half an hour we would be having our first marital argument.

Well, you know what they say, 'Start as you mean to go on'.

# CHAPTER THIRTEEN

## Fight Club

We arrived back at Frank and Sheila's and they put the kettle on as we all felt the need for a brew. We went to get out of our wedding finery and back into our normal comfy clothes. After our brew, my lovely new husband decided he wanted to open the wedding presents now. I said it wasn't a good idea as, once we'd opened them it would be twice as hard to get them all in a taxi to go home. He argued that it would be ok as we could leave all the wrapping behind but Frank chipped in and said we weren't leaving our rubbish in his dustbin, we could take it home with us. Sheila joined in, then Cheryl had an opinion and before we knew what was happening a full-scale row was in progress.

We hardly ever argued before we were married, just the odd tiff that soon blew over but here we were, married for three hours and fighting like cat and dog. He was shouting that nobody would tell him what he could do with his own presents, he wasn't going to be a hen-pecked husband. Meanwhile I was yelling back that just because he'd got a ring on my finger didn't mean I was going to turn into a doormat. It was insane.

It went on for a bit longer before he put the final nail in his own coffin,

"You're just like your mother" he yelled.

Instantly the room went quiet, the other three were holding their breath waiting for the bomb to drop. Even he realized he'd said the wrong thing there but he wouldn't back down. I was quite dignified in my response, I said I didn't want to argue in front of his family but once we got to our own home I was going to rip his head off for saying that.

Then Sheila rang for us a taxi quickly, before I changed my mind and we started stacking the presents near the front door ready to go. When the taxi came, they helped us load it up before Sheila said, "See you tonight then".

"You might do" I replied and then we drove off.

We didn't speak for the first ten minutes of the journey but then the taxi driver found out we'd just been married and was full of congratulations and everything. It all started to feel a bit silly, who wants to kill each other over a few stupid presents.

When we got home we both said sorry. I said I wasn't bothered about him arguing over presents but it might take a bit longer to forgive him for the 'mother' thing. He said he didn't mean that, I was nothing like my mother then we set about opening the offending presents.

Twenty minutes later we were wondering why we had ever bothered arguing over such a strange assortment of stuff. We had been given more ash trays then we knew what to do with, only one of us smoked and would never need that many ash trays. One of them was a massive onyx one that weighed a ton. I can't remember who bought it for us but I remember six months later I dropped it on my foot and had a black toenail for months.

Most of the stuff was for the kitchen and we had to keep referring to the boxes to see what it all was. Didn't these people realize I had been raised in my mother's kitchen, the only thing I knew how to use properly was a chip pan. Some bright spark had given us a fondue set. Is there law that someone has to buy you one of these when you get married? Everyone seems to get one but nobody I've met has ever used one. Never mind, if we hid it away we could give it to Cheryl and Alistair for their wedding. Maybe there are only a few fondue sets in the world after all, they just keep getting passed around to newly-weds from the ones that came before them and didn't know what fondue was.

I'm pretty sure a lot of what we'd been given was second hand and had been kicking round at the back of someone's cupboard for ages. We also seemed to have quite a few hideous ornaments, I have never been an ornament person and have never felt the need to have skating teddy bears and fishing frogs dotted about on my shelves. I had the thought that a lot of our Christmas shopping was already sorted for that year.

Vicky's parents had bought us a stainless-steel kitchen set with teapot, milk jug and sugar pot, egg cups and salt and pepper pots. It must have been quality because thirty-six years later we still use the salt pot every day. Pretty much everything else was gone by the time our first anniversary rolled around.

We didn't have much time to get ready before the night time 'do' started. For some reason, we had to be there first to welcome our guests. I didn't see why, as far as I could see we were the important people that day. Surely, they should all be there first to see us make our grand entrance. Apparently not, so we rushed to get ready again, forgetting that we hadn't eaten all day (we didn't really bother with the buffet, we were too busy entertaining). We dashed off to consume lots of alcohol on empty stomachs, it was asking for trouble.

When we arrived at the club the DJ was just finishing setting up, Frank and Sheila arrived just after us with Cheryl and Alistair. They were looking out for Anne, who was being forced once again to be 'happily married' for the evening. They didn't want her and the best man that nobody liked turning up separately and arousing suspicion. My parents arrived not long after that, without my brother who was at home with Joan and sleeping off his hangover.

A bit later, on all our friends started piling in. Now we could have a proper party, the DJ turned up the music and the real wedding party got under way. It was a really good night, everyone was having a great time drinking and dancing. Every time the pair of us turned around someone else was pushing a drink into our hands. There were lots of drunken toasts going on.

Even the oldies were all up on the dance floor having a boogie, which is where things started to take a turn for the worse. I noticed my Auntie Dolly was up dancing with my new grandad but I couldn't see nanny. I found her after a while in the ladies' toilets, crying into her hanky. When I asked her what was wrong she said grandad had found another woman.

What woman, where? She described my Aunty Dolly. I laughed and told her not to be daft, they were only dancing, Aunty Dolly was dancing with everyone, that's what she was like. Nanny said she'd seen it in his eyes, after fifty years of marriage he was going to leave her. I got Cheryl to look after her while I went to talk to the love birds.

On the way, I bumped into Anne who was getting her coat on. She said she was sorry but she was sneaking away, she couldn't spend another minute pretending she was still with that moron down there. We had a big hug and I told her I didn't blame her one bit, she said she'd already found her little bro and told him she was going. I told her to get off before Frank and Sheila noticed she'd gone.

After she'd left I went in search of Grandad and his new woman. They were still on the dance floor, having a whale of a time. Aunty Dolly was totally unaware that she was in the middle of breaking up the marriage of a couple of pensioners who had already seen their golden wedding anniversary come and go. When I told them that Nanny was upset Aunty Dolly felt awful, she said they were only having a laugh, Uncle Malcom was only a few feet away. I thought Grandad would say the same but then he blurted out that he was under my Aunty Dolly's spell.

"What"? Aunty Dolly looked at me, obviously confused.

"Your Aunty Dolly has enchanted me" grandad said. I realized either he'd drunk a few too many Pils or my Aunty Dolly had some strange power over men that I'd never been aware of before. Either way Aunty Dolly was looking decidedly uncomfortable. She thanked Grandad for dancing with her and made her escape quickly.

Cheryl was bringing her Nanny back out from the toilets, she looked better now but she also looked mad. She took grandad off to one side for a quiet word in his ear. I spotted Frank and Sheila looking around for Anne, I think they had realized by now that she had gone. The best man that nobody liked had gone as well and it was obvious they hadn't left together. They started bickering about it.

When I started looking around I realized the mood had changed quite a bit. It was getting really late now and everyone had been drinking for a long time. I noticed a few little squabbles going on, Nanny was bending Grandad's ear about Aunty Dolly, Vicky and Derek were having words because he was ready to go and she wasn't, Frank and Sheila were blaming each other for not being able to control their daughter. Even my parents seemed to be having a disagreement over something, I could tell by the fixed party grins on their faces and the heated whispering.

I went to find my new husband only to be met by him demanding to know where I had disappeared to, he said he had been looking all over for me. I told him he can't have looked far as I had been sorting out his grandparent's marriage problems on the dancefloor. There were a few more little exchanges and then suddenly we found ourselves back in the middle of the wedding presents row again.

This time some of his friends jumped in to take his side so my friends who were mostly their girlfriends started telling them to keep out of it. Before we knew it, half the guests were involved in some sort of quarrel with somebody over something. Someone must have tipped the DJ off because he turned the music down and bid everyone goodnight.

Everyone crowded round to collect their coats and started ringing taxis. Most people were decidedly worse for wear by now, it had been a really long day. We stopped bickering and said goodbye to our families and everyone else. We only had to walk to the top of the street to get home but when the fresh air hit us

I realized my husband was a lot drunker outside than he had been inside. We set off for our house, bickering again because he was so slow and I wanted to get home.

At the bottom of the street we had to cross the big iron bridge that went over the railway lines. There were loads of steps up, a short bridge then lots more steps back down. Half way there my very drunk by now husband decided he couldn't go any further. We got the rest of the way home by me pushing and dragging him down the other side of the bridge and then down the terrace to our house.

When we finally arrived, I did the traditional thing of kicking him over the threshold then he staggered off up the stairs to bed, while I went to put the kettle on. Before he went he told me how much he loved me and that I was the best wife in the world. He had obvious forgotten that ten minutes before we were threatening to throw each other off the top of the bridge.

I left him to it and went off to drink my tea, ten minutes later I heard him snoring like a wounded pig. What was this? I had never heard him snore before, I had stayed at Frank and Sheila's loads of times. Why had I never heard this before? I started to think Frank and

Sheila had passed him on to me under false pretenses.

I came to the conclusion that this marriage lark wasn't all it was cracked up to be. Still half-drunk myself, I decided I would wait until morning then go back home and have a rethink. A minute later I remembered my bed had been sold and by morning my brother would have claimed my old room. Oh well, better make the best of it then, I finished my brew then made my way upstairs to claim my half of the marriage bed before he was sick in it.

By the next morning, it was all forgotten. To be fair we had both been as bad as each other. I thought we must be the worst married people ever but over the years, of all the married people I have met, ninety per cent of them had the same experience as us. I think it must be the stress, after all the months of planning, preparation and trying to keep everyone happy, combined with exhaustion and far too much alcohol.

We started our married life properly that day now that we had no more outside interference (and we had sobered up) and got on fine together from then on. Well until the next row anyway. We put most of the presents out of sight and enjoyed our first and last honeymoon day. Tomorrow we had to go back to work and normality, we were grown-ups now, it was time to face up to our responsibilities.

Oh, and by the way, he wasn't sick in the bed.

# CHAPTER FOURTEEN

## Our Happy Home

Back at work the next day I lost count of the people who asked me if I felt any different now that I was married. I still had a bit of a hangover and far too many boxes in my dustbin but that was about all. All my friends said I wouldn't be allowed to have my breaks with them now that I was an old married lady. They said I would have to sit with the other married women and talk about recipes and how to get rings off wooden coffee tables. I told them I didn't cook and my coffee table was glass.

The only thing I wasn't looking forward to was going home to an empty house. My husband was still working the two to ten shift so he wouldn't get home until ten thirty, it was starting to get dark early now and I didn't like the idea of going home to a dark empty house. After a few weeks, I got used to it, Fridays we worked until after eight so I didn't get home until late then anyway.

About two weeks after the wedding we had been presented with our wedding pictures. Most happy couples are given a big fancy wedding album, we were given a paper packet from Boots the Chemist. Let's just say they weren't brilliant. There were a couple of nice ones that we could have enlarged but the rest looked like holiday photos. I didn't think Gerry had much of a future as a wedding photographer.

We had properly settled in to our little house by now and had filled it with all our stuff, it was starting to feel like home now. We still couldn't believe how cheap the rent was and thought it was really nice of Frank and Sheila's friend to let us have it for that just because they were friends. Little did we know.

Because the shop I worked in wasn't far from my parent's house I still went there most days for my dinner. Miss Turner went home every dinner time too and passed their house so she started giving me lifts in her little old car. This was a most surprising turn of events. She treated me a lot nicer now that I was married, even though it had only been five minutes. She even started telling me a bit about her life, up to now apart from her church and boys brigade stuff all I knew was that she lived with her sister and brother in law.

One day she told me sadly that she had never married because she had met the love of her life and he was already married to someone else. She never looked at anyone else after that. I felt sorry for her and began to feel bad for hating her for so long, she was lonely and must have felt even worse, watching everyone around her finding someone and settling down when she never would. I wouldn't say we were friends and she still had her moments but when we were on our own she was a lot better.

The nights began to get darker and our little house began to get colder. One Friday night I arrived home in the dark at about nine o clock. I went in and put the lights on and I was just going through to the kitchen when I heard a bang from upstairs. My first thought was that there was someone up there. We didn't have a phone in that house and there were no mobiles back then so I couldn't call anyone. I didn't know any of the neighbours, they had all eyed us suspiciously when we moved in and then kept to themselves.

There was no way I was going to go up there and look and I wasn't going to stay downstairs and wait to be murdered either so I kept my coat on and went out to sit in the front garden until my husband came home. I sat there for over an hour, freezing until he came around the corner. I ran to tell him we had an intruder upstairs so he started looking for a weapon. Someone had bought us a set of brass fire tools (even though we only had a gas fire) as a wedding present so he grabbed the poker and went off upstairs to bash the intruders head in. I waited downstairs and waited for the shouting to begin.

Instead I heard him laughing and talking to someone, he shouted for me to come up and meet the intruder. I crept upstairs, wondering why he was having a conversation with him instead of beating him to death. When I peeped around the bedroom door, he told me to 'meet the burglar'. Instead of the big scary man I was expecting, there was a big fat tabby cat stretched out on our bed. He had been prowling around the dressing table and had knocked a load of things over. That was the noise I'd heard. He must have sneaked in earlier in the day and got locked in.

I recognized him as the cat from next door so I picked him up to take him home. I knocked on the door and explained to the woman who answered what had happened. Instead of seeing the funny side and thanking me for bringing him back, she said she'd been looking for him all day and accused me of cat napping. What a cheek.

My intruder had given me an idea though, I would get a cat, that way I would have some company when I came home and, because my husband didn't leave for work until the afternoon it wouldn't be on its own all day. The next weekend we took ourselves off to the cat's home and came home with our first child 'Fluff'.

He quickly settled in and made himself at home. When I came home at night he would be sitting in the bay window waiting for me, then at quarter past ten every night he would scratch at the door to go out. Then he would sit on the back wall and wait for the sound of my husband's motorbike. As soon as the bike slowed down at the corner he would jump down off the wall and on to the pillion seat where he would sit while my husband drove down the terrace and into the hallway (it was a massive hallway, so I let him keep his bike in there out of the weather). He was a very smart cat.

Towards the end of November, we realized all was not as it seemed with our little love nest. To start with it was freezing all the time but we put that down to us having been pampered for years with central heating. When the slugs started turning up in the bathroom though that was something we weren't expecting. The first time they turned up I thought I was still dreaming.

I had got up, put the kettle on and then gone into the bathroom to get washed. As I opened the door my first thought was that someone had been squirting shampoo all over the floor, there were slimy trails everywhere. On closer inspection, I realized they were slimy slug trails and, worse still, the slugs that left them were all over the bathroom. They were all over the floor, up the walls, in the sink, I had never seen so many slugs, not even in my dad's garden. I didn't know they even came out in winter, and what was so special about my bathroom.

I ran screaming upstairs and dragged my husband out of bed to show him. He spent ten minutes rounding them all up and throwing them back outside. That seemed like a bad idea to me, they would just slither back in for a warm up. I cleaned all the slime up and carried on getting ready for work.

After that, every morning was the same, I started having to get up early to do a bit of slug wrangling before breakfast. We bought loads of bathroom sealant and blocked every gap that we could find but still, every morning they were back. I'm sure they were the same ones every day, eventually I started naming them, Slinky, Fatty, Odd-Bod, the list went on.

My dad told me to throw salt over them every day to kill them all off but there was never enough salt to cope with them all. Plus, when I did that I had more mess to clean up, slime and salt. For some reason, they only liked the bathroom, they never showed up in the kitchen. In the end, we gave up trying to kill them off and we all lived together.

The weather got a lot colder really fast. One morning we woke up and the bedroom window was covered in ice. Not too strange, you might think, but it was on the inside of the glass, it was like sleeping in an igloo. We bought an electric blanket, which made going to bed a lot easier and warmer but made getting up torture.

Towards the end of November, we noticed that a lot of the neighbours were starting to move out. Every other day there was another removal van pulling up outside and, by the end of the day another empty house. One morning as I set off for work the next door neighbours were moving all their stuff out.

"Are you moving now"? I asked the woman (the same one who had accused me of cat napping).

"Yep" she said, "Got our keys last week, when are you going"?

I didn't know what she meant, why would we be going, we'd only just got there.

Then she told me that all the houses were being pulled down. Everyone had got their notice last year; the council were giving them all new houses.

This was a complete shock to me, how come the rent woman hadn't mentioned this when she had given us the keys? I ran back inside and told my husband. He said he would find out what was going on before he went to work, there was nothing I could do so I carried on and went to work.

All morning I was worrying about what would happen, would we get keys to a new house as well? Just before dinner time he rang me at the shop.

Apparently, our house had a compulsory purchase order on it and had done since the year before. The council had bought it from the landlord and it wasn't to be rented out any more. There was worse to come. Because we had moved in after the compulsory purchase order had been given, we weren't entitled to a new place from the council. We weren't actually supposed to be there at all.

No wonder Frank and Sheila's 'friend' was letting us have it cheap, she was making herself a few quid on the side. I couldn't believe it, we were going to be homeless.

At dinner time, I went to my mother's and rang Sheila at home to tell her. She was as shocked as we were, she immediately rang her friend who admitted that she had 'slipped up', she should never have given us the keys. Sheila told her we wouldn't be paying her any more rent and that was that, if she complained we would tell her boss what she was up to. I wanted to tell her boss anyway. We had known it was too good to be true.

That night when my husband came home from work we decided we weren't moving out. We had nowhere to go anyway, there were no decent places to rent, only grotty flats and bedsits. We figured if the council wanted us out they would have to give us somewhere else to live.

So, started a campaign of letter writing that went on for weeks. The council said they wouldn't give us anything and we had to be out by March when the demolition was due to begin. We kept telling them we weren't going anywhere. After all, they couldn't start demolishing the street with us still in it, could they? At least I hoped not.

Then we began blackmailing the council, if you want to pull down our house, give us some keys. What could go wrong?

By Christmas there were only two other houses still occupied. When January came around they moved out and we were on our own. My dad told us to give up and find somewhere else but I told him I would make banners and have a sit-in if I had to. This terrified him, it would get in the papers. People would think I was an activist.

Because everyone else had gone, all their water had been turned off. This meant that we had practically no water pressure at all. When we turned the taps on there was barely a trickle coming out and flushing the toilet was a nightmare. We discovered a trick to doing this though. We found out if we bounced something up and down on the plughole in the bath at the same time as we flushed the toilet, it somehow gave the toilet enough temporary pressure to flush. It was quite a feat and usually took two people, we found the best way was to stand in the bath and put one foot over the plughole.

If anyone was coming to visit us we had to tell them to 'go' before they got to our house as it could prove embarrassing if we had to run into the toilet just as they had finished and jump in the bath. Not surprisingly, we never got many callers.

When February rolled around the council turned all the street lights off. This meant every night when I came home from work I would have to walk home in complete darkness, it reminded me of the power cuts a few years ago. They were really stepping up their campaign to get us out now. It was so cold in the house by this time that even poor Fluff had ice on his whiskers and Stinky, Fatty, Odd-Bod and the other slugs were frozen stiff in the morning when we went into the bathroom to stand on one leg in the bath.

This wasn't how we'd pictured our first few months of married life. At least we had plenty of cuddles though, we had to cuddle a lot, it was the only way to stay alive. The two of us and Fluff in the middle. I knew if the council turned the gas off as well we would be done for.

Towards the end of February, just as I was considering taking my story to the local paper, a letter dropped through the door. Our postman didn't like us as he had to walk half a mile out of his way, down empty streets just to deliver our mail. This morning he had brought us some news, the council had backed down. Because we were holding up their plans they decided to give us somewhere to live just to get rid of us. We had won.

We had to go straight to the council's offices to pick up some keys. It turned out they were only giving us a flat but it was a modern one, with central heating and a flushing toilet. We would be warm again, we could stop going to the bathroom in tandem and people would visit us again.

The flat was on the same estate as Frank and Sheila but it was quite a way from them. It was in the same building as Anne's flat and we would be living just across the landing from her. We started packing the same day.

A week later the removal van turned up and we left quickly before the demolition ball began swinging. Before we left I popped my head around the bathroom door, took one last look at the bath that I would never have to stand in again, and said farewell to Stinky, Fatty and Odd-Bod. I hoped they would find somewhere else to live before the walls came crashing down onto them.

# CHAPTER FIFTEEN

## Love is Blind

We felt like we were in Paradise in our new flat. We had forgotten how it felt to be warm and to be able to turn on the taps and see water gushing out, even better, hot water. I lost count of how many baths I had in the first week. We said we would never take our comforts for granted again but we soon got over that.

The only down side was I still had to take two buses to work every day, just from a different direction. Now we had the motorbike though I was able to get lifts home some nights, much to my parents' disapproval, they didn't like motorbikes.

After a few weeks, we realized that we wouldn't be able to keep Fluff. It wasn't fair to him to keep him locked up in a flat all the time, he had a litter box but he wasn't happy, he wanted to be able to go outside again. One of Anne's friends said she would take him so, sad as it was, we let him go. I was going to ask my mother for the address of the farm where she had sent all my pets over the years but I was afraid I wouldn't like the answer.

We quickly got stuck into decorating the flat and went out to buy wallpaper for the living room. Neither of us had ever done any wallpapering but I had watched my dad enough over the years to know what not to do. In the end my husband said he would start it while I was at work as it was a 'man's job'. I resisted the urge to kick him in the goolies and let him get on with it.

The next day I set off for work and he assured me it would be half finished before he left for work himself at one o clock. I came home at teatime excited to see how it looked. It looked like someone had run amok in a wallpaper factory. There were little bits stuck here and there and the rest of it was torn into tiny pieces on the floor. Across the bare wall he had scrawled, 'This paper don't work'. Apparently, he wasn't such a good decorator after all.

When he came home that night he explained that it wasn't him, it was the paper, it wasn't cut straight. When it met at the top it gaped at the bottom and visa-versa. I went along with this and said I would take it back and complain. On my next day off I went back to the shop and picked a different paper, throwing the rest of what we had left down the rubbish chute on the way. I would tell him the shop agreed with him, it was faulty paper.

I took the paper home and when he had gone to work I had a go myself. I found it quite easy and by tea time it was half finished. It was quite a relief to find out I hadn't inherited my dad's DIY skills. From that day to this I have done all our wallpapering, even when he tries to help, my other half is useless at it. He went on to become a plasterer and he was brilliant at it, he could get walls as smooth as glass with his trowel but wallpapering remains a complete mystery to him. He just can't do it. So much for it being a 'mans' job.

Now that we were living on the same estate as practically everyone else that we knew, we saw a lot more of our friends. My husband's best friend (the one who hadn't been good enough to be best man) lived a couple of blocks from our flat. I had never been to his house or met his family so one day we popped for a cup of tea. My husband said his friend had lots of brothers and sisters and it was probably going to be a bit of an eye opener for me. I wanted to know what he meant but he just laughed and told me to wait and see.

When we got there, I was a bit nervous and didn't know quite what to expect. We knocked on the door and his friend Stuart opened the door and told us to come in. When we got inside I didn't know what to think. At first I thought they must be moving out, they didn't seem to have any furniture, just a couch and a few stools. Stuart's mother came out of the kitchen to say hello and my first thought was that she must be his grandma. She looked about sixty-five and she was only about five feet tall. Then his dad came in behind her and he looked even older, and maybe a bit smaller, also he was limping really badly. I later found out he only had one leg and his false leg didn't fit properly so it was always falling off.

Stuart's mother seemed really glad to see my husband, I mean really, really, glad. She launched herself at him to kiss him hello and was determined to land her mouth on his. He did a lot of ducking and diving and in the end she missed and got his ear, at the same time he was trying to slap her hands away as they kept grabbing at his bum. To say I was shocked was an understatement. I didn't know whether to laugh or slap her for molesting my husband. Eventually she left him alone, said hello to me and said she would put the kettle on.

Then there came the sound of feet thundering down the stairs and five children of different sizes came running in. They all squashed together on the one couch and proceeded to stare at me as if they had never seen another person before. I was staring back at them, probably more intensely, I couldn't quite believe the sight before me. Although they were different ages they all had identical faces, not only were their faces identical to each other, they were also identical to the little banjo player from the film 'Deliverance'. It was uncanny.

I came to the conclusion that their parents must be very closely related, there could be no other explanation. I shot a look at my husband to see if he knew what I was thinking, he was laughing his head off. "Told you" he said. Just then his other woman came in and told us to come and have our tea in the kitchen, she had found two kitchen chairs from somewhere. I sat perched uncomfortably on one of the chairs, peering at my tea and trying not to judge these people. I didn't want to look down on them like my parents would, they were very friendly and asking about our new flat and how our parents were. Stuart looked really uncomfortable, I could tell he was ashamed of where he lived and must have been wondering what I was thinking.

Stuart's mother (her name was Gladys) shouted the children through into the kitchen to get their hands washed before they had their dinner. They all trooped in, still staring at me. I smiled at them and one of the girls, who must have been about twelve came up and stroked my face. I was stunned, I felt like the first white woman must have felt among the natives in the jungle hundreds of years ago. Then she whispered that she thought I was pretty, bless her. I said thankyou and told her she was too. She giggled and then lined up at the sink with the others to wash her hands. I was thinking it couldn't be that bad here, they were hygienic anyway.

That thought went away though after they all dried their hands on the kitchen curtains. I couldn't believe my eyes. I finished my tea and we said we'd get out of their way so they could have their dinner. Gladys told us to come back anytime, we were always welcome, then she tried to kiss my husband goodbye while he made a dash for the door. She gave me a peck on the cheek and said how lovely it was to meet me, then I caught sight of her husband limping towards me with his arms outstretched and a glint in his eye. That was enough for me, I elbowed past my husband and I was out the door and up the path before his wobbly leg could get near me.

Once outside I demanded to know what the hell had just happened, were they real people? My husband said that's why Frank and Sheila didn't like Stuart, because of his family. I asked if Stuart was adopted, after all he didn't look like the 'dueling banjo' kids. He said no, Stuart and his older brothers were all normal, something had happened after they were born and the next lot of kids all came out like that. I couldn't imagine what could have happened but it must have been something serious. I thought I would probably have nightmares for a week after that.

We never went to Stuart's again after that but I often bumped into his family when I was out shopping and they were always nice to me. Eventually, the kids stopped staring at me and started talking to me, they were quite sweet really. A few years later Stuart met a nice (normal) girl and they got married and had two kids. I have always wondered what she must have thought when he took her home to meet his family. She must have really loved him to marry him and risk having kids when she was fighting those genes.

Stuart and my husband were always messing around with engines, bikes and cars. Our flat had come with a big garage so now they had plenty of room to tinker around. I was forever trying to get oil stains out of his jeans.

One day he bought an arc welder. He said they could weld all sorts now and he couldn't wait for Saturday so he could try it out. He went off out to the garage as soon as he got up. The welder came with goggles, a mask and a warning not to use it without wearing them. I stressed to him how important it was to use them and he promised he would.

He was in the garage practically all day, messing around and getting filthy. He came in before tea, had a bath and then we settled down to watch telly. Later on, we went to bed.

In the middle of the night, half asleep, I heard him saying,

"I'm blind, I can't see". Now he was and still is terrible for talking in his sleep, I have been awoken in the middle of the night hundreds of times over the years by him spouting rubbish, I have learned to ignore it and sleep through it. I thought that's what was happening now, so I just said something along the lines of,

"That's nice, go back to sleep". I heard him get out of bed so assumed he was going to the bathroom and went back to sleep myself.

A few minutes later I awoke and realized he wasn't there and he wasn't in the bathroom. I looked out of the window and saw him, stumbling along the walkway outside, arms outstretched like a little kid playing blind man's bluff. He was heading for his sister

Anne's flat, I didn't know if he was sleepwalking or what so I ran out after him.

He wasn't sleepwalking, and he really was blind, he couldn't see a thing. The silly sod had been using his welder without the mask or goggles. He was on his way to Anne's to get her to ring a taxi to take him to hospital, we were still waiting for our telephone to be fitted.

We knocked on the door until Anne woke up. She was a bit surprised to say the least to find her brother on the doorstep at three o clock in the morning, and even more surprised to find he was blind but she rang us a taxi. I led Ray Charles back to our flat to get our coats and then, when the taxi came we set off for hospital. I was in a state of panic, what if this was permanent, how would we manage? He was clumsy enough already with two good eyes, stumbling around with a white stick he would be a liability. I would have to leave work to look after him, how would we manage?

When the taxi driver heard what had happened he said he had seen this load of times before, it was just a welding flash and they would sort it out at hospital. He told us not to worry. I thought that was easy for him to say, he wasn't the one who would have to look after a bad tempered blind person. I would spend the rest of my life describing what was on the telly. I'd said for better or for worse, I just wasn't expecting the worst to turn up quite so soon.

When we arrived at the hospital the taxi driver was proved right. They whisked the poor blind bugger away into a room and put some drops in his eyes. When he came back out of the room he could see again, it was a miracle.

We had to spend more money on a taxi home again, I could have cheerfully throttled him. Why did he think they put warnings on things and what was the use if you were just going to ignore them? Like a typical man, he never takes notice of things like that. Whenever we buy anything with instructions he never reads them. I have lost count of the things he has put together without looking at the instructions. Without fail, every time he has finished, he always has a pile of things left over. He says you don't need them, they're just spares. Over the years. he has accumulated enough of these spares to build ten more of whatever hc was building in the first place.

# CHAPTER SIXTEEN

## Don't Scratch

It was now 1979, summer had rolled around again and in a couple more months we would be celebrating our first wedding anniversary. And they said it wouldn't last. Our flat was all finished now, nicely decorated (thanks to me), with all the comforts of home. Our latest purchase was a state of the art music centre. This sounded grander than it actually was. It was a record player with built in radio and cassette player, it looked really cool though, long and slim with a smoked glass top. We thought we were dead posh. I had recently bought Blondie's album 'Parallel Lines' and I played it non-stop for months. I played it so much in fact that I wore it out and had to buy a new copy.

This was the year I decided to get a perm. A couple of years before, the film 'A Star is Born' starring Barbara Streisand had come out. Me and all my friends had been to see it and wept buckets, we had all also been dead impressed with Barbara's bubble perm. Some of my friends had run straight out and got one but I was a bit more wary. I had experienced too many disasters with my hair in the last few years so I decided to leave well alone.

Now, a couple of years later, I decided to go for it. There was a little hairdressers next door to our shop and I knew the owner, Cathy quite well as she was always in our shop. The only problem was she closed at the same time we did. One day she said she would do my hair for me after work when she had closed up so when I had finished for the day I went round to her shop. She locked the door behind me and set to work. After a while she suggested we have a glass of wine, it was past tea time so it was quite respectable. She cracked open a bottle and we drank while she transformed me into Barbara, without the nose.

It took ages and we had just about finished the bottle by the time she was done. When I looked in the mirror I could see why she had wanted to get me drunk before she showed me the end result. Instead of Barbara Streisand staring back at me in the mirror, I found myself looking at Vera Duckworth. It wasn't at all like I had imagined it. Cathy said not to worry, in a few days it would 'drop'. It looked like it might drop out, when would I learn to stop fiddling around with my hair? Not for another fifteen years but I wasn't to know that then.

A couple of months before this we had been given some good news. We were to become an Aunty and Uncle after Christmas. Not long after our wedding Anne had met someone new, around the time we had been given our flat he had moved in with her and now they were pregnant. As soon as her divorce came through from the best man that nobody liked, they were going to get married. His name was Terry and he was really nice but a bit quiet, he didn't really know us all properly yet.

Imagine the pickle Frank and Sheila were in. They wanted to brag to everyone that they were about to become grandparents but they also faced having to explain to everyone that Anne was pregnant to someone else when, as far as they all knew, she was happily married. Serve them right for lying.

Anyway, back to my hair, after a while I found out that Cathy was right, my perm 'dropped' after a bit and began to look more like I had intended in the first place. It looked better the more it grew out and I didn't regret it so much anymore. I do now though when I look back at photos from that time.

One Sunday towards the end of August I woke up feeling quite ill, it felt a bit like having flu. I took paracetamol and waited to feel better but instead, as the day went on I was feeling worse. By early evening I was feeling so bad I didn't know what to do with myself. My husband rang his mother for advice and Sheila popped round. When she saw me she said my temperature was sky high and I needed a doctor. She got straight on the phone to the emergency doctors. By this time, I would have happily paid anyone to shoot me, I could hardly stand by now and I was starting to come out in blisters all over.

When the doctor arrived, he took one look at me and said that I had Chicken Pox. What, how could I have Chicken Pox? That was a little kid's illness. He asked if I had them as a child, when I said no he said,

"There you are then, you've got them now." He said I would be off work for two weeks and contagious for ten days. I was horrified, I would be all itchy and scabby and I would have to ring in work and tell Mr. B. He would never believe me, nobody my age got Chicken Pox. Before the doctor departed he told me not to scratch or I would get scars. Great, more good news.

The next morning, I rang in work to tell them I wouldn't be in, Debbie answered the phone. I told her to get Mr. B.

"Why, what's up?"

"Just get him."

Mr. B came on the phone and I told him my news. He took it like I expected.

"You've got what?"

"Chicken Pox".

"That's a kid's thing."

"Well I never got it when I was a kid."

The phone went quiet for a bit, I heard a bit of whispering then Debbie laughing her head off,

"She's got what?"

Then more laughing. I was glad she found my predicament so amusing.

Mr. B came back on the line and I told him I would be off for two weeks and I had a sick note to prove I wasn't making it up. He said ok they would see me in a couple of weeks, just before he hung up he gave me a bit of advice.

"Don't scratch, you'll get scars."

Thanks for that.

I should have been happy to get two weeks off work but I was bored to tears. Because Anne was only just over three months pregnant she had to be careful so I had to stay away from her. That meant I had to stay away from the rest of the family as well in case any of them carried my germs back to her. I couldn't ring any of my friends for a chat because they were all at work. I felt like I was in prison. Aunty Dolly rang every few days to see how I was doing and when we had finished chatting she always said goodbye and reminded me,

"Don't scratch, you'll get scars".

To make things worse it was boiling hot outside and I was stuck in the flat. Our windows ran the full length of the living room wall and even though we could open them all it still felt like a giant greenhouse. I sat watching rubbish telly all day while trying not to scratch my spots.

My mother popped round every few days with shopping and things. She brought endless supplies of calamine lotion and told me not to scratch my spots or I would get scars. I was heartily sick of hearing that by now, every person that said it thought they were telling me something I didn't know, even the postman had told me the day before. My mother also brought me jigsaws to keep me amused but I wasn't that bored. My family was big on jigsaws, the more pieces the better, they liked a challenge. I could never really see the point of them, you spent all those hours, scrabbling around for the right shaped pieces and sorting sky from sea and grass from trees and what for? You ended up with the same picture as was on the front of the box, it was hardly a surprise. Then, after all that, you broke it all up into pieces again. Well, most people did, my family liked to keep their efforts. When they finished one that they really liked they glued it onto a board, framed it and hung it on the wall.

Whenever I asked them why they bothered they would say they liked the picture. In that case why not just cut the one off the front of the box and frame that? It would save all that time and effort. They just said that wouldn't be the same, obviously missing the point that it would be exactly the same, just without all the wiggly lines.

Instead of jigsaws I asked my mother to bring me some wool and knitting needles and I set about knitting some baby things for my soon to be niece or nephew. My mother had taught me to knit when I was young and I was ok at it. Probably not as good as my little brother had been but his knitting career had been cut short the day my dad caught him knitting and purling. My mother was read the riot act and he wasn't allowed to do it anymore. It was a shame really, I think he found it relaxing after a hard day spent Avon collecting.

Later on, he moved on to cross stitch and one of his masterpieces was framed and hung on the wall along with the jigsaws. My mother would point it out to visitors and my dad would tell them it was a school project and he had been forced to do it. It didn't help much though when, whenever my mother told my brother to,

"Show them your embroidery."

After over a week of forced imprisonment I could take no more. My spots were more like little scabs now and had stopped itching so, one morning I slapped loads of make up over them and took myself out shopping. I felt like I had been let out of a cage, and spent ages going shop to shop looking at all the things I usually took for granted. I didn't think I was still contagious but I wasn't sure, I was living dangerously. My mother said I was being a 'silly girl' but she had been saying that for as long as I could remember and I had never taken any notice.

When the two weeks were, up I couldn't wait to get back to work. Everyone was really glad to see me back but only because they had all been sharing my workload. Debbie had even been roped in and shown how to do the cheese. At long last, I had an assistant.

Every other customer seemed to know all about my chickcnpox, they all wanted to know if I had been scratching (a bit personal I thought). When I said no, I had covered myself in calamine lotion they all said that was good.

They didn't know if I had heard but if you scratched your spots you would get scars.

# CHAPTER SEVENTEEN

## Now Here's an Idea

By the time September rolled around everyone had heard about Anne's news. Frank and Sheila had found some way to tell everyone without making themselves look bad. All the women in the family were furiously knitting away and the jackets and bootees were piling up. I thought Anne could probably open a market stall, flog it all and use the money to buy baby clothes that she really liked.

Our first wedding anniversary was only a couple of weeks away, the first year had flown by. Every other person was asking us now when we would be getting a 'little addition". I told them we had already had one but we couldn't keep him in the flat so gave him away. I really should have told them I meant the cat but some of their faces were a picture.

What with everyone asking all the time and seeing Anne and Terry getting all their things ready it started to make us think. We were proper grown-ups now, we were making good money, why didn't we consider joining Anne's pudding club. We had already proved what good parents we were to Fluff, and since I had almost killed my brother by letting his pram roll down a hill eight years ago I hadn't caused any harm to any other child. I was a model citizen now.

We thought about it for a while and then decided we wouldn't actually 'try' to get pregnant, we would just let nature take its course and see what happened. After all, I had heard it could take a year or more before it happened. So that's what we decided. I stopped taking the pill and we left it to fate. We agreed not to tell anyone because they would only keep quizzing us to see if anything had happened yet, and it would probably be months before anything happened if at all.

So that was it, it was all in the hands of Mother Nature now, she would decide if sometime in the future she would bless us with a 'little addition' (a baby not another cat). With that, we agreed to put it out of our minds and we went about our daily lives.

You can imagine the scene six weeks later when we were both sat gob smacked, looking at a positive pregnancy test result. Mother Nature was obviously more impatient than we were. I kept thinking there must be some mistake while my other half got all over excited and renamed himself S.S. (Super Sperm). I refused to call him this, it lowered the whole tone.

Now we had to tell our families. We went and told my parents first, my dad, bless him did his usual trick of blushing bright red and mumbled something about 'costing him an arm and a leg', I knew he was dead chuffed really. My mother said she knew it, she knew that coat was getting too tight round the middle. Cheek, I hadn't put an ounce on yet I was only a few weeks gone.

Sheila's reaction was even stranger, she said for the last couple of weeks she had thought something was going on because my nose had changed shape. Apparently, it was 'more pointy' which was a sure sign of pregnancy. To think, all that money wasted inventing pregnancy tests when all you had to do was look in the mirror at your nose. What if your nose was naturally pointy though, did you go through life with everyone assuming you were pregnant?

Frank said I should sit down and put my feet up for the next eight months, I said I would try but my boss would at some point probably make me stand up again and get back to stacking the shelves.

Anne was dead excited as well, now our kids could grow up together, they would be the same age. Cheryl said she was jealous, she and Alistair had got married six months after us.

Their wedding had been a lot more peaceful than ours, they had seen all the fighting at ours and said they weren't going to drink and spoil their wedding night.

Because they weren't drinking, out of politeness everyone else watched their alcohol intake and so there was no bitching or unpleasantness between people. It was a nice day, but compared to ours it was boring.

They had a flat near Frank and Sheila and, like we had been, were parents to a cat who they named Mabel. Cheryl said she would love to be pregnant but that she didn't think it would happen yet as they were still 'having trouble getting that bit right'. The mind boggled.

Vicky and Melanie were very excited to be future 'aunties'. They both said they would buy me baby clothes as they were both crap at knitting. Melanie was still working in the bank but Vicky had left her job to work in a massive medical supply factory. She was working on a 'line' where things came down a conveyer belt and she and the other workers had to pack things together for medical kits. It was piece work, which meant the more you packed the more money you earned. She told me they all tried to go really fast but it was hard to keep the pace up, especially if someone down the line was a bit tired.

One day she told me that little problem had been fixed. One of the girls' mothers had been put on slimming tablets from the doctors but didn't like them. She said when she took them she couldn't sit down for more than five minutes and they stopped her sleeping. She gave them to her daughter who took them to work and every morning all the girls on the line took one each. For the rest of the day they would fly through their work, thousands of medical kits were put together every shift, she said they even asked if the conveyer belt could be turned up to go faster.

This was all because back in those days slimming tablets were filled with nothing but amphetamines, they were all taking massive amounts of speed. Nowadays they would all fail the drugs tests and be fired, back then they were the best employees in the factory. Vicky was earning a fortune and she said as an added bonus she was slimmer than she had been for years. I knew she would be a model 'auntie' and a real inspiration to my child. Look what you could achieve with hard work, and class B drugs.

When I told everyone at work about my news they were all delighted. Miss Turner said that's what God intended and Mr. B told me not to forget to book that day off as I had with my wedding. I was still in shock, I never imagined it would happen this fast.

When we worked out the dates out we figured it must have happened almost straight away. I thought back to Halloween, all us girls from work had gone out for Debbie's birthday and it had been quite a hectic night, I had been pregnant then and not known it.

There were about eight of us altogether. We had spent the first part of the night in the same German pub where my engagement party was held, it was where everyone went for their birthdays. We were under strict instructions from Debbie not to try and involve her in any 'party games'. She would not, under any circumstances be on that stage dancing, singing or humping balloons. We said absolutely not, she didn't have to worry about anything like that. Then the minute she went to the loo we put her name down for all three and even told the compere where she was sitting in case she got under the table to hide.

When she came back we had a few drinks, stood on the tables for a bit of singing and waving glasses around, then we sat down and tried not to notice that the chairs were being arranged on the stage in a row. The balloon humping/popping contest was about to begin. We all feigned surprise as the compere came to our little group and took Debbie by the arm, he was taking no chances of her doing a runner. He announced over the microphone that it was her birthday and everyone cheered as he wrestled her onto the stage. She put up a good fight but the man was used to throwing out drunks and was stronger than he looked.

He shoved her into a seat that was already fitted with her balloon and pump, a load of the usual women took the other seats, (there were quite a few exhibitionists in there all the time) and the 'oompah' music began.

It was one of the funniest sights I have ever seen. Debbie, humping up and down furiously as the balloon between her legs got bigger and bigger, with a face like thunder. If looks could kill we would all have been dead and buried in 1979. On the plus side she won the contest, she was so desperate to leave the stage she humped twice as fast as the other women so her balloon popped first.

After she had been given her prize, a ticket for free entry for a month (which she ripped up and threw at the compere) we realized it was time to go. We tried to convince her it was nothing to do with us, the bar staff had overheard us talking and told the compere it was her birthday but she wasn't having any of it. In the end, she calmed down enough for us to convince her to let us take her to the nightclub across the road. We promised we would pay for everything so she relented, she said she would forgive but not forget. I thought none of us would ever forget either, it was too funny.

We hadn't even realized it was Halloween until we got into the nightclub. It wasn't very big in Britain back then, nobody ever went trick or treating or dressed up in those days. The first we knew of it was after we had paid our money, it was a quiet night in the club as it was mid-week. We walked down a corridor towards the double doors at the bottom, the corridor had been decorated with cobwebs, bats, spiders and stuff and dotted about were statues of ghosts and monsters. We carried on down the corridor, still laughing about Debbie when, all of a sudden, as we passed an open coffin, the body inside it came shuffling out of it and came towards us. I thought I would die on the spot, we all screamed and ran back the way had come in. The 'body' started laughing and got back in the coffin,

"Gotcha" it said as we composed ourselves and turned to head into the club again.

We were giggling and telling each other how we weren't expecting that, Debbie said she didn't think she could take any more that night. We got to the end of the corridor and up to the double doors that led to the bar and dance floor. Just as we were about to open the doors, a curtain at one side of them was flung back and a zombie jumped out and grabbed at us. Debbie wasn't kidding when she said she'd had enough, she turned around and punched the zombie in the face.

"What did you do that for"? yelled the 'zombie', holding its face.

"Because it's my bloody birthday and I want leaving alone" screamed Debbie. None of us could believe it, we never knew she had that much bottle. This was one night out we would remember.

Now that I had worked my dates out I realized I was getting all these shocks and scares at the most delicate time in my pregnancy. Well it looked like my future little 'addition was one tough cookie.

Back at work, word had leaked out to some of the regular customers and they were joining in with Sheila's mad theories. Apparently one lady could tell I was expecting straight away as my eyes had gone closer together. Was this person mad, how could someone eye sockets and eyeballs one day just up and move an inch closer to each other?

I couldn't believe what I was hearing but more was to follow. Another could tell by my chin, which was rounder than it had been the week before. Someone else said I was walking differently. They were all nuts but each one was deadly serious when they told me, they really believed it.

It got so I was scared to look in the mirror. With my pointy nose, round chin, odd walk and wandering eyeballs I would have looked right at home in the 'walk of horrors' we had seen on our night out at the club.

And I was only six weeks gone.

# CHAPTER EIGHTEEN

## Peep Show

I was about four months along now and still waiting for my bump to pop up. I bought maternity clothes that buried me and stood on buses, one hand on my back, belly sticking out, waiting for someone to take pity on the poor pregnant lady and give up their seat. Nobody ever did. I think they just thought I had really bad posture.

In the last few weeks I had been getting horrendous morning sickness, I was fine first thing in the morning. It would show up at around eleven o clock, just as we were sitting down for tea break at work. I had to sit there watching everyone else stuffing their faces with chocolate biscuits and guzzling down tea while I sipped Lucozade, nibbled on a dry cracker and tried not to heave. I wanted to ask Miss Turner if this was what her god intended, as she had told me, how long did he intend this bit to go on for?

In the end, it lasted for another month, it was probably the worst part of the whole pregnancy. Everyone had little remedies that they all swore had worked for them but none of them worked for me, I just had to wait it out.

At about three months I had been for my first examination, I had been terrified about this prospect as I had been told to expect an 'internal examination'. I was so traumatized at the thought of this that I sought advice from Jill, one of my older workmates who already had two children. She laughed at me and told me.

"What are you worried about? It's no different to what you let your husband do, only he doesn't wear rubber gloves."

I had no idea what she and her husband got up to in the privacy of their own bedroom but after I had been and had it done I could never look her husband in the eye again when he picked her up from work. Every time I saw him I pictured him wearing marigold gloves with a light strapped to his head while Jill waited behind him with her legs in stirrups.

It seemed like the world and his wife were knitting for me, customers kept bringing me little knitted things which was very sweet of them and back home the clothes were piling up. Anne was almost due and she had everything she needed now so everyone was knitting for me. Because we didn't know what we were having, most people stuck to white and sometimes lemon. Cheryl decided to be a bit different and started bringing me garments in weird and wonderful colours. One day she turned up with a little cardigan which was two-toned in orange and chocolate brown.

It was so much like the things my mother used to make for me it was spooky. I started to think back to the years when I was convinced I was adopted. I had always suspected as well that my mother might have accidentally swapped me during one of her 'special' days. Now things started to fall into place. Me and Cheryl were the same age, born a few weeks apart, we had grown up a few streets away from each other and our mothers used the same shops. It was perfectly reasonable to think that my mother could have parked Cheryl outside the shop and come home with me. Maybe Cheryl was my mother's real daughter, hence the strange knitting. I had always felt that I was in the wrong family. Sheila probably wouldn't have noticed either as both of them were about as good as each other in the mothering stakes. The more I thought about it the more it made sense. Just as I started to panic at the thought that I might be Frank and Sheila's real daughter I thought back to my Aunty Dolly's sensible words. She had been there when I was born and always told the tale of the birthmark on my bum. Every time I pestered her about being adopted she would ask me,

"Have you still got the birthmark?"

"Yes."

"Which cheek."

"Left one."

"There you are then you daft bugger, you're the same person I saw pop out of your mother, now go home and stop mithering me."

She was right, I still had the birthmark and I knew for a fact that Cheryl didn't have any birthmarks as I had asked her before.

I was who I was supposed to be and the mad knitting was just a coincidence. It never even crossed my mind until later that if I had turned out to be Frank and Sheila's long- lost daughter, I had just got pregnant to my long-lost brother.

Thank god I had a birthmark.

At about five months along I was sent for a scan. I had to have it done at the maternity hospital, or as I called it, the cattle market. It was an awful place, run by awful nurses who treat everyone like dirt. On my first visit, they had called my name out as 'Miss'. When I told the nurse I was 'Mrs.' not 'Miss' her reply was,

"Just in time eh?"

Charming!

At the hospital, everyone was herded around like cattle and treated with no dignity whatsoever. After your name was called you were all sent to sit in a long corridor to wait for the doctor to see you. They had a notice on the wall that said,

**"Please remove your tights and underwear while in the waiting room."**

Honestly, we all had to sit in the queue with our knickers in our handbags. One time when my husband was working and couldn't come with me I took Cheryl. She read the notice and then asked me,

"Do they mean me as well"? She was never the sharpest tool in the box.

When I went for the scan my husband came with me, in those days husbands stayed in the waiting room, they weren't involved like they are today. I was sent into a cubicle, dressed in a hospital gown and told to follow the nurse to the scan room. Unfortunately, they had run out of the robes that went over the gowns and as a result I went waddling up the corridor with my bare bum hanging out of the back of my gown. Ever the gentleman, my husband didn't bother jumping to my rescue to cover my modesty (and birthmark), he sat and laughed along with everyone else in the room. He never even told me about it until three weeks later but by that time I didn't care, any dignity I had possessed was long gone. By now I had lost count of the people that had peered at my bits. One time while I lay with my legs in the air a whole class full of students filed past one by one for a look.

When the nurse did the scan, she pointed to a little bag and said that was baby's bladder,

"Aah" I thought.

Then, suddenly, the little bag deflated really quickly, the nurse said that was baby having a wee,

"Ugh" I thought. I didn't know babies weed before they were born.

After a bit more scanning, the nurse brought a doctor and they both looked at the monitor, humming and haahing and completely ignoring me. When I asked if everything was alright the doctor actually shushed me, then he said,

"Young lady, you've obviously got your dates wrong, you are not five months along, you're only about four".

I told him no I hadn't got the dates wrong and my doctor had confirmed my pregnancy when I first went to see him five months ago. He told me I was wrong again, the baby was too small for five months. I let him have his opinion but I knew I was right.

Patronizing old git.

I went home with a new due date that I took absolutely no notice of.

Shortly after that Anne's divorce from the best man that nobody liked came through and she and Terry slipped off on their own and got married.

A week later I became an Aunty for the first time in my life. Anne and Terry had a baby girl, my first ever niece. She was lovely but very demanding and over the next few weeks proved to be quite a handful, she was a bit of a baby drama queen, crying all the time until she got her own way. She's over thirty now and still the same way. We did a bit of babysitting to get in some practice for our own impending arrival but it didn't go well. We ended up frightened and wondering what the hell we had let ourselves in for.

People kept on telling me not to worry, it was different with your own. I hoped they were right.

A few days after the scan I was at work on the checkout when one of the regular customers came in waving the local paper.

"You're in here" he shouted to me, you're famous."

"What are you talking about?" I asked him "I haven't done anything."

"Oh, yes you have." he chortled, showing me the paper. To my horror there was a big photograph of me and my husband, Anne and Terry, Cheryl and Alistair and Frank and Sheila. I recognized the photo, it had been taken at Frank and Sheila's silver wedding anniversary in their living room. The headline read,

**"Family getting bigger all the time thanks to magic beer!"**

I thought I must be dreaming.

When I read the article, it was about how me and Anne had become pregnant within weeks of each other after drinking the special beer at Frank and Sheila's favourite German pub in town. It also said Cheryl and Alistair were regulars there so were expecting to hear good news any time now. Apparently, the pub had secret ingredients in their beer and anyone who wanted to have a baby soon should pop in for a pint or two. I knew exactly what was going on, the pub was on its last legs and was due to be closed down soon. Frank and Sheila weren't having any talk of closure and they were doing whatever they could to drum up publicity for the place.

I was mortified, they hadn't even asked for our permission. I knew my dad would be horrified as well, he had lived in fear of one of us getting in the papers for years. At least it wasn't for anything criminal, it would be though when I got my hands on my in laws.

For the next few days all the customers were cracking jokes all over the place, some of them even asked for my autograph now that I was famous. I couldn't wait for it all to go away.

Frank and Sheila thought it was great. Anything they could do to stop 'their place' closing down they would. Sheila said when that pub opened it gave them both a new 'leaf of life.' She was always getting her words mixed up, once she had to have an E.C.G on her heart and went around telling everyone she had been for her G.C.E's. My own mother wasn't much better though, she once went to buy some textured paint called Sandtex. She went into B&Q and asked the man where they kept the Semtex. They must have thought she looked like the world's most unlikely terrorist.

My husband inherited his mother's mixed up speech. He always comes out with the wrong words, although by now I usually know what he's on about. Recently we were talking about how we always know what the other is

thinking or what we're about to say before we say it, he said it's because we've been married so long now we have become psychotic.
He could be right.

# CHAPTER NINETEEN

## Tales of Terror

I was now more than six months gone and only now was I starting to get a little bump. Up to a fortnight ago I had still been wearing my normal jeans and people who didn't know me had no idea I was pregnant. I could definitely tell now though as my bump had started moving around. The first time it had happened it made me jump, it felt really strange. The film Alien had been released the year before and Wayne had gone into great detail in the tea room about the alien bursting out of John Hurt's stomach. I hadn't seen it yet but every time my bump moved I was reminded of Wayne's descriptions. I wished he had kept them to himself.

I only had a few weeks left at work now and was mostly sticking to working on the checkout. Now that I didn't have much time left the customers started imparting their words of wisdom again. If I had thought their opinions on how to tell you were pregnant were strange, what with changing eyeballs, noses and whatever, I hadn't heard anything yet. This time it was only the female customers and they were regaling me with tales of labour and childbirth. It was both terrifying and screamingly funny at the same time.

Everyone knew someone with a horror story, one lady told me that her sister's husband's cousin had been in labour for seven weeks with no drugs or painkillers and that she had eventually gone mad and killed the doctor.

Someone else's boyfriend's mother's aunty had gone for a wee one day when she was seven months gone and the baby had slipped out unnoticed and she had flushed it away. When she saw my horrified face, she said it was ok, there was a happy ending, because the baby was still attached by its umbilical cord she just pulled it back from round the u bend and it was fine.

On and on they went, every story more unbelievable than the one before. There were three legged babies, babies with tails, babies that were both male and female, other babies that were neither. The old ladies who came into the shop all told exactly the same story, every single one of them knew of a woman years before who had given birth to a seventeen-pound baby who was born with a full head of hair and three teeth. By the day after he was born apparently, he was eating the same meals as his mother. I hoped it was the same woman that they all knew of or there must have been a lot of older ladies who were walking around like John Wayne.

It got so bad that I was scared to go to sleep for fear of the nightmares I might have.

When they weren't trying to frighten the crap out of me with tales of agonizing, body wrecking childbirth, they were predicting the sex of my baby. They all had different ways of telling. I had needles and cotton suspended over my belly, wedding rings dangling on bits of string, once again my nose was called into the matter. Apparently, it was certain to be a boy because the bridge of my nose was wider than before. Dear god what was the matter with my nose, it was pointy at one end and wider at the other, I figured after this baby was out I should stay in hospital and wait for a plastic surgeon to sort it out, while he was at it he could put my eyeballs back into their original position.

People looked at my feet (your second to big toe gets longer if it's a girl), my fingernails were scrutinized (ridges mean it's a boy), and my hair was a big focus of attention. Everyone knew if your parting got wider it was a boy, either that or you were just going bald from the stress of all these mad people.

One old dear was doing the suspended wedding ring trick over my belly one day, she said if it spun clockwise it was a boy, anti-clockwise meant a girl. Off she went, it spun one way,

"It's a girl. Oops, hang on it's going the other way, it's a boy. No, wait it's a girl. Ooh maybe it's twins, one of each."

I just hoped it wasn't one of those babies that the other women told me about, the baby that was both. What colour would you dress one of those in?

Back at home it was my husband who was getting the unwanted attention. Another woman had her eye on him. It had started a couple of weeks before when I was at home on my day off. There was a knock on the door and when I answered it a little girl was standing there, she looked about nine years old.

"Hello" she said.

"Hello" I answered.

"Is your boyfriend in?"

"Do you mean my husband?"

"Yes, is he in?"

"No, he's at work?"

"What time does he get home?"

"Not until after your bedtime. Why?"

"I think he's lovely."

"Right, well he's a bit old for you, isn't he?"

"I don't care."

I thought this conversation had gone on long enough, so I told her to go off and play and not to think about boys until she was a bit older. She said she was off to the shops with her Grandma anyway and skipped off. I thought no more of it. When my husband came home later we had a laugh about it and that was that.

What we didn't realize at the time was that this little girl could have given Glenn Close from Fatal Attraction a run for her money. The next night I had just got in from work. Me and my bump were just putting our feet up when there was a knock at the door. I dragged myself up and opened it, there was the little girl again.

"Hello."

"Hello, what do you want now?"

"Is he in yet?"

"No, I told you he doesn't get in until late and he won't want to talk to you anyway."

"I'm going to marry him."

"No, you're not, he's already married."

"When I'm old enough I'll marry him."

Good god she was persistent. I wasn't going to stand here fighting with a nine-year old over my own husband so I told her to go home.

"I'll come back on Saturday when he's in." she said.

"Don't bother, I called after her."

She smiled and waved and skipped off again.

When Saturday came around, sure enough there she was on the doorstep again.

"Hello."

"Hello again, what do you want."

"Is he in now?"

"Yes, but he's having his dinner."

"What's he having?"

"Chips."

"Can I have one of his chips?"

"No, bugger off."

"Please, can I have one that he's bitten?"

This was getting too weird now. I told her no, she couldn't have a chip and if she didn't go away I would have to tell her mother.

"She already knows."

"Knows what?"

"That I've found a boyfriend and I'm going to marry him, she laughed and said ok."

I didn't think she'd be laughing when she found out her daughter's little boyfriend was twenty-two and already married with a bump on the way.

"Look, enough's enough now, you're starting to be a nuisance now go home". I said.

She was unfazed.

"I think he looks like a pop star." she said.

"I don't care what you think, bugger off." I said, closing the door.

I went back inside.

"What the hell have you done to get so much attention from a nine-year old?" I asked the pop star who was hiding in the kitchen.

"I don't know, I don't even know what she looks like, I didn't know any little kids were watching me." He sounded quite nervous and I didn't blame him, we didn't know how big this little stalker's father was.

"It's not my fault I look like a pop star." he laughed.

Funnily enough, this had happened before. Once, a couple of years before when we were coming out of the cinema, we had been chased down the street by a couple of teenage girls who were convinced he was 'that singer from Smokey'. His hair had been a lot longer then.

After that, whenever there was a knock on the door he would run into the kitchen whispering,

"I'm not in."

It was always my job to get rid of her after telling her, no, she couldn't have one of his chips, socks, or anything else. In desperation one day I told her we didn't have time for this nonsense, we were having a baby.

"Can I look after it when it's born?"

"No, now go away."

She never got the message or went away insulted. Every other day she was back, desperate to get a glimpse of her heart throb.

One Saturday afternoon when we were in the supermarket doing our weekly 'big shop' I saw her coming up the aisle with a woman I assumed was her mother. Because my husband had no idea who she was he didn't do his usual thing of hiding. The first he knew of anything was when this little girl pointed at him and shouted,

"There he is mam, that's who I'm going to marry."

I don't know who looked the most shocked, my husband or her mother. Actually, I do, it was her mother. She dragged her daughter away and whatever she said to her when she got her home must have done the trick. She never knocked on our door again. It was quite a relief, I could come home from work again, safe in the knowledge that I wouldn't find my goldfish boiling away on the stove. (I know 'Fatal Attraction' didn't come out until years later, I put that bit in for comic effect.)

# CHAPTER TWENTY

## I'm Right, You're Wrong

It was my last day at work. I was seven and a half months along by now so I only had six weeks to go. That was according to my reckoning anyway. The patronizing doctor at the cattle market was still insisting I had my dates mixed up and I was only six and a half months. I knew I was right. His argument was still that the baby was too small to fit in with my dates and that I hadn't put enough weight on.

He might have been right about the weight, I had still only put on just over half a stone, I figured I was having a petite baby, after all, I wasn't exactly a big person myself. I knew from the time that my bump had started moving that I was right. I would show the patronizing doctor when the time came.

Before I left work for the last time I was given quite a few gifts from the customers and a big baby basket from everyone at work, full of bottles, rattles, little toys, bibs and things. It was really nice of them and I promised to bring my bump in to show everyone once he or she put in an appearance. Leaving for the last ever time was quite emotional and I felt really sad to be going. Still, I couldn't stay on much longer, Mr. B was getting more nervous by the day, worried I might give birth on the checkout.

I came home from work that last night and wondered what I would do with myself for the next six weeks. Everything was ready for when the time came, I only had to pack a bag for the hospital and I thought I would do that in a couple more weeks.

For the next few weeks I pottered around at home, visited my mother and Aunty Dolly and saw my friends when they had a day off from work. The weather turned really hot in mid-June when I only had about four weeks to go. At the same time my bump suddenly took off, people who hadn't known I was expecting now realized and started asking me where 'that' had come from. Where did they think?

As it was so hot and my bump had got so much bigger I was dead uncomfortable, it was hard to get any proper sleep and every time I lay down I got terrible heartburn. I wanted it to be over now.

One night I was reading the paper after tea, trying to get comfortable I had put the paper on the floor and was leaning over it looking at the telly page. Suddenly a few drops of blood dropped onto the newspaper, my nose had started bleeding. This was new, I had been told that my nose was pointy and wide but nobody had mentioned anything about it bleeding.

My husband immediately went into a panic, what if it was high blood pressure, what should he do? I said I was fine, it wasn't much but he rang the doctor's number.

"Hello, my wife is pregnant and she's bleeding." I couldn't hear the other side of the conversation.

"She's nearly eight months along."

"No, not that much, it just suddenly fell out onto the newspaper."

By this time, I was realizing that he hadn't told them I was bleeding from my nose. I started trying to tell him he hadn't told them that bit.

"No I don't think she's getting any pains."

"Now she's holding onto it and squeezing it, she's tipping her head back."

By now I figured the poor woman on the other end of the phone was getting confused. She must have asked him what I was holding and squeezing and why I was sitting on newspaper. I couldn't imagine what she was picturing.

I thought I should probably take the phone myself now and put this poor woman straight. I took the phone away from him and told the woman I was fine and it was just a nosebleed. My husband had panicked that was all. She said that was ok, she had heard all sorts from expectant fathers and to ring back if I needed anything.

I started to get a bit worried, if he panicked like that over a little nosebleed what would he do when the proper thing started?

Over the next few weeks the weather kept on getting hotter and I was getting more uncomfortable by the minute. Whenever we could we decamped to my parents' back garden for some air, it was stifling in our flat even with all the windows open. I was still stuffing myself into my strappy sundress from last year. Up until a few weeks ago it would have still fitted me (just about) but now I looked ridiculous. I couldn't zip it up anymore so I walked around with the zip half down at the back. Although I looked odd it was nowhere near as bad as my show at the clinic when I flashed my bum to half the waiting room.

Two weeks before the date I thought I was due I had another appointment at the hospital. Once again Dr. Patronizing told me I was further away than I thought. He poked and prodded my bump around and then went for his rubber gloves, I didn't think it was because he was going to do a bit of cleaning. I was right.

After a bit more prodding he asked if I had experienced any 'leaks'. I was sorely tempted to tell him there was a bit of a puddle in the cupboard under the sink at home but I was already on his naughty list because I wouldn't agree with him over the dates.

He got his pen out, had a bit of a whisper with the nurse who was with us and then started furiously writing in my file. I asked him what was going on and he actually said the words,

"It's nothing to do with you."

I wanted to borrow his rubber gloves and give him a taste of his own medicine.

When he had finished writing he told me to come back in a week's time for another appointment. I gathered my dignity and my knickers and took myself off home again before he could patronize me any further.

That was on the Monday. On the following Saturday, my cousin Janice was getting engaged to her boyfriend and they were having a big party. We went along while we still had the chance, in another few weeks we would have to get a baby sitter before we could go anywhere.

It was a really nice party, there were loads of people there and it seemed they all wanted to stroke my bump and talk to it. The drunker people became, the more they held conversations with it. It was quite bizarre as it couldn't answer back. I wondered if they would have talked to my belly if I was just fat and not pregnant.

We got home quite late and went to bed tired out, at least the next day we could sleep in as it was Sunday. The next day was very quiet, we didn't go out and just sat around the flat watching telly. We went off to bed about eleven o clock. I had my appointment at the hospital the next day and I was dreading it. According to my reckoning I only had twelve days left but I knew Dr. Clever Dick would tell me that was wrong and I still had another month on top of that.

Around three o clock in the morning I was awoken by a slight pain in my stomach. I lay awake for a bit but it stopped so I went back to sleep. About an hour later it happened again, I looked at the clock to start timing things and half an hour later I had another twinge. It wasn't terribly painful so I put it down to wind or indigestion, I had quite a craving for ice cream in the last few weeks and I had eaten loads before I went to bed.

Every half an hour I got another twinge, after a couple of hours they started to get more painful. I didn't bother waking my husband up. I waited until about eight o clock in the morning before I told him. He wanted to know if this was it, should we go to the hospital? I said I didn't think it was labour pains, more likely to be wind and anyway, I would be at the hospital in the afternoon anyway.

A couple more hours went by and the pains were getting stronger, I had seen women on telly going into labour and they always seemed in a much worse state than I was in. I shouldn't really have compared TV dramas to real life though, the last woman I saw giving birth on telly had somehow managed it without taking her dungarees off first, or even undoing the shoulder straps for that matter.

I decided I would ring my mother, she would know what labour felt like. I dialed her number and when she answered I asked her.

"What does labour feel like?"

"How the bloody hell do I know"? she screamed. "It's been years since it happened to me and everyone knows as soon as its over you forget what it felt like."

Really? Nobody had told me that, it was the first I was hearing of it.

"Stop buggering around and get to hospital" she said "You might not have long to go, when did it start?"

"Three o clock this morning." I said.

The sound coming from the phone sounded like an air raid siren. She was panicking a lot more than I was. I told her I would keep her posted and rang off.

My husband was desperate for me to go to hospital by now, I think he was frightened we might not get there in time and he might have to deliver his own child by the side of the road. I had once seen him helping a cat give birth to kittens and he faffed around like a demented midwife during that. I think the poor cat was quite annoyed with him, she was managing quite well on her own before he showed up and started tearing the bags from her kittens before she could.

I decided we would put my bag in the car just in case but that we would drive to Frank and Sheila's first to get their opinion. By now I had been getting pains for over six hours. We got in the car and headed off to their house, on the way the pains suddenly got stronger and more frequent.

By the time we got to their front door I was starting to wish we had just driven to the hospital. Sheila opened the front door to find me curled up in a ball on the doorstep.

"What does labour feel like?" I gasped.

"Oh, my god you silly bugger, probably something like that. Get back in that car and get to hospital, NOW!"

I figured she might be right so we did an about turn and headed back to the car.

We arrived at the hospital at around lunchtime and went straight to the labour ward, Sheila had already let them know we were on the way. My husband was sent to the waiting room and I was wheeled into an examination room. The nurse prodded me about and then asked me how long I had been getting pains, I told her it was around nine hours by then.

She went away for a minute and came back with another nurse who also had a prod about. She asked me when my waters had broken and I told her they hadn't. She said they must have, if not, where were they? How the hell was I supposed to know? They were the midwives, not me. They asked if I had felt like I had done a 'really big wee'. I told them no, I might not be an expert like they were but I'm sure I would have noticed if half a gallon of liquid had suddenly exited from my nether regions.

I could tell by the way they were looking at each other that they thought I was a simpleton. Then one of them asked why I hadn't come to the hospital sooner.

"I thought it might be wind." I told them.

They looked at each other again as if this confirmed what they had been thinking and I saw them both roll their eyes. They weren't exactly subtle. One of them confirmed that I was definitely in labour and the other one went to page Dr. Patronizing.

When he arrived, he took one look at me and said:

"You are determined to prove me wrong about these dates, aren't you?" As if I had done this deliberately.

He joined the prodding club, then out came the gloves again. When he had finished that he took the nurses to one side and they all commenced talking about me behind my back again. I was straining to hear what they were saying but all I could make out was

"Too soon" and "One leg."

Oh, my god, I was having a one-legged baby. All the tales I had heard from the customers at the checkout came rushing back. I tried to butt in and ask what they were on about but once again I was shushed like a naughty toddler.

Dr. Patronizing came back and confirmed that I was in labour but he said because it was a month too early he would put me on a drip to try and stop it.

He was determined to win this bet.

I was wheeled off to a side room and the nurses came in and started fiddling around getting a IV fitted to the back of my hand. When they were done, they let my husband in to sit with me and said they would monitor me every half an hour.

As soon as I saw him I told him the news, our child only had one leg. He told me not to be daft, if that was true they would have picked it up on the scans. I made him go off and find out anyway.

He came back ten minutes later and said that I had heard wrong, there were definitely two legs in there.

I instantly decided he was lying, he was in on the plot to keep it from me. No matter what he said I didn't believe him. It was a conspiracy.

For a while it looked as if the drip was having an effect (the IV drip, not my husband), the pain was definitely subsiding. Dr. Patronizing was delighted, he was right. For a while I thought he might start dancing around singing,

"Told you so, told you so."

It didn't stop for long though, after about an hour with nothing, the pains returned stronger and they were more frequent now. The nurses went off for the doctor again and when he came back he seemed most annoyed with me.

He told me since I was determined to do this today I would have to be taken to the theatre. I felt like saying thank you but I was in no mood for an evening out. He said I would need a caesarean because my baby was breech, which was something else they hadn't told me. Upside down and one legged, this wasn't anything like I had imagined.

They started getting me ready to go for my operation, they were so busy plugging things into me and pulling other things out I didn't really have time to be scared. Just before they wheeled me away a nurse told me when I woke up my baby would be in an incubator as she was so small. Aha, 'she' I don't think the nurse realized she had just given the game away, before that we didn't know what sex the baby was.

My husband was sent off to the waiting room again, he looked more scared than me.

Before he went they asked him what I was like on anesthetic, he said he didn't know, I had never had any operations since he had known me.

I had only been given anesthetic a couple of times before at the dentist but I knew both times I didn't have good reactions. Apparently, I had become violent, not that I remembered anything about it. I took after my mother for this, she had once had a tooth out and, while coming round had set about the dentist, kneeing him in the testicles.

On her way, out she had stepped over him writhing in agony on the floor. The next time she needed an appointment he was 'full up'.

Once my husband had been sent out I was put onto a trolley to go off to the operating theatre, someone stuck a shower cap on my head and off we went. When we arrived, I was put onto another table, someone placed a mask over my mouth and nose and told me to breathe deeply. A few breaths and I felt myself slipping off (to sleep, not the table).

This was it then, when I woke up again I would be a parent, probably to a very small, one legged little girl.

# CHAPTER TWENTY-ONE

## Here's One We Made Earlier

I was trying to wake up but it was hard to get my eyes open. I was dimly aware of somebody slapping my face but I couldn't seem to raise my arms to slap them back.

Where was I?

After I managed to get my eyes open, my first thought was it must be the United Nations as, hovering around me were lots of faces, all different colours. There was a white one, a black one, a brown one, a Chinese one, they were all talking at once.

Then I realized, I must be at the dentist but I couldn't remember getting there. I struggled to speak.

"How many have I had out?" I asked.

"Just the one." laughed the Chinese face.

"What are you going to call her?"

I didn't know what she was on about, why would I name a tooth?

I tried to sit up and a horrible pain shot through my stomach. Slowly, things started to come back to me. It was over, I wasn't pregnant any more. I looked round, first for my one-legged child and then for my husband.

The nurse told me my baby had been taken to the nursery until tomorrow. They wanted me to rest for the night before they put us together. Then they told me that there had been no need for an incubator. She was small but not that small, five and a half pounds. I had been right she said, I was only around ten days early. I knew it!

When I enquired after my husband she said they would let him back in shortly, when the security guards had finished with him.

"What?"

Apparently, I had behaved just like my mother on the anesthetic, I had screamed the hospital down, shouting to everyone that I was being attacked. My husband had burst in through the doors to help me and ended up being tackled by the guards who dragged him out again. He wasn't very amused when he realized I was just hallucinating. I had no memory of any of it.

When they had sorted me out they let him back in and left us alone. He said he had just been down to the nursery to see our new arrival and she was small but perfect. I didn't believe a word and asked him about the one leg. He swore on his mother's life that he had seen two legs.

I still wasn't convinced, I knew he wasn't all that keen on his mother. I came to the conclusion that everyone was giving me the night to get my strength back before they broke the news to me in the morning. In desperation, my husband asked the nurses if he could wheel me down to the nursery to see for myself. They said no, I couldn't be moved yet. More proof I thought.

It might seem stupid now but at the time I really believed my own delusions, it must have been the hormones (and the drugs).

After a few hours, my husband went home for something to eat, he came back later with my parents in tow. My mother was going on and on about how beautiful the baby was. I told her it was ok, I knew she only had the one leg. I saw her shoot a look to everyone else, I thought the look meant,

"Oh no, she knows." when in fact it meant, "Oh no, she's lost her marbles."

When visiting time was up, they all went home having failed to convince me that I was bonkers. I didn't know why they wouldn't just admit it, I had resigned myself to having a one-legged daughter by now and I wasn't upset, I was trying to think of practical things.

What she had never had, she wouldn't miss and all the socks and bootees would last twice as long as I would only be using one at a time.

I slept for quite a long time, waking up at about three in the morning. An orderly was passing my room and saw that I was awake, she said she would get me a cup of tea and a biscuit. She asked where my baby was.

"In the nursery." I told her "She's only got one leg."

This poor woman sat with me for ages telling me how brave I was and not to give up hope. She said the doctors could do marvelous things with little false limbs nowadays, at last, someone who didn't tell me I was mad.

I bet she felt daft the next day, I know I did.

The next morning someone brought me some breakfast and said when I had eaten it they would move me onto a ward, we would stop on the way to pick up the baby from the nursery. She would have a cot by my bed.

When I was ready they put me onto a trolley and wheeled me off down the corridor to the nursery. They parked me up while someone went into the nursery and came back holding a tiny little thing wrapped in a blanket.

"Here she is at last." said the nurse, handing her over.

I couldn't believe how small she was, no wonder my bump hadn't been very big. The first thing I did was peel back the blanket to see for myself. There, under the blanket were two legs, as legs go they were tiny but there were two of them. I started to feel very foolish.

The second thing I checked was her left ear. All my husband's family had a massive left ear that stuck out more than the other. From the back, they all looked like taxis with one door left open. To my relief she had my ears, that's about all she got from me, everything else looks like it's been cloned from her dad.

Apart from being small, she was perfect, she didn't look like a premature baby at all. I think my first words to her, before I introduced myself were,

"I knew I was right."

We were taken to a room at the end of the ward where they were keeping all the women who had caesareans. There were four beds in it and I would be sharing with three other women. In those days after the operation they kept you in for ten days, five in the hospital and then another five across town in a special 'after hospital' to recuperate.

You weren't allowed out of bed for the first few days, not even for a wee. It was totally different back then. A few years ago, after my niece had a cesarean she was up and around the first day. She said they insisted on it.

I had a small see through cot next to my bed for the baby, the nurse put her in it and said she would come back in a bit to show me how to feed her and do the nappies, which were toweling ones. Disposable nappies were only just coming out back then and they were nothing like they are today.

Some of the nurses were already treating me a bit huffily because I was bottle feeding instead of being a 'natural mother'. Over the next few days I watched these natural mothers trying to get the hang of it. It seemed to be a proper kerfuffle, the babies couldn't do it properly and ended up being hungry and screaming all the time. In contrast, my child was fast asleep with a full bottle in her belly, burping contentedly.

That seemed more natural to me.

For the first few days the pain from the operation was horrendous, every time I tried to even move my legs it was agony. Laying down to sleep was impossible, we all had to sleep sitting up, propped up by loads of pillows.

Every four hours or so the nurse would come in and give us all a shot of Pethidine in our bums, the effect of this was remarkable. One minute we were these agony ridden women, too frightened to move a big toe in case we pulled on our scars, huddled under the sheets, in too much pain to even talk. The next we were proper party animals, babbling away non-stop, laughing and singing and trying to get up for a dance.

I thought this Pethidine stuff was marvelous, we all did. One night when visiting time was ending I tried to walk my family out to the car park, which didn't go down well with the nurses. I was told in no uncertain terms to get my Pethidine filled bum back into bed.

After three or four days, I was going mad with boredom, the weather was still hot and we could see everyone sunbathing through the windows of our little prison. I had plenty of visitors, Frank and Sheila came with Cheryl a few times, my Aunty Dolly and Janice came and my parents popped every other day, my husband came every day. I still wanted to get out.

On the fifth day, we were all shipped out to the other place to spend our last five days, it was quite a shock. Instead of being in a little room we were all split up and put on one long ward. There were about thirty women, all with babies that screamed at different times of the day and night so it was never quiet. Now we were here we were encouraged to get up and walk around. That would have been alright but at the same time they stopped all our painkilling drugs. We were told that the only things we were allowed here were two paracetamols.

Were these people mad, didn't they realize we were dependent on hard drugs now?

They probably did and that's why they stopped them after five days before we all became raving addicts.

On my second day there I was just finishing my dinner when who should I see doing the rounds but my old adversary Dr. Patronizing. I wondered if I would get an apology for all those months of arguing about my due date. Surely, he would admit now that I was right. I couldn't wait for him to get to my bed to see my not premature baby.

He didn't have the bottle to face me. He went around every bed and then when he got to mine he put his head down and walked straight past me. Huh, patronizing and ignorant as well, what an idiot. I was dying to shout after him,

"Yoohoo, I was right wasn't I?"

By the afternoon of that second day I had more than had enough. I was in so much pain I couldn't think straight and for all the good they were doing me there I might as well have been at home.

Then I had a brainwave. I rang my husband and told him to bring some of my dad's strong painkillers at visiting time, my dad took them for his arthritis.

When he turned up I took a couple and then waited for them to take effect. Within half an hour the pain was lots more bearable, I shouted for the nurse and told her I was going home, I was going to sign myself out. She tried to talk me out of it but as I had my daughter under one arm and my bag under the other she realized my mind was made up. She brought the necessary forms and I signed them, then she escorted me from the premises. It felt more like getting thrown out of a pub than leaving hospital.

Once in the car we headed to my parents' house for a cup of tea before we went to our own home. Unfortunately, by the time we finished fiddling about at the hospital and made it through the traffic my painkillers were starting to wear off.

This meant that by the time we pulled up outside of the house I couldn't move my legs again and so I was trapped in the car. It was still hot so we opened all the car doors and my mother brought tea and biscuits out to the car

Joan from next door and all the other neighbours heard that I was there and they all wanted to see the baby. The result was that we had quite a little street party, I entertained from the back seat while the baby was passed around everyone and given gifts and money. It went on for about an hour. My dad was once again mortified, I was making a show of us again and now I was dragging his grandchild into it as well. He kept telling my husband to take me back to the hospital but he told him that because I had walked (staggered) out, they wouldn't take me back again.

After a while I took some more painkillers with my tea and we set off for home while they were taking effect. The neighbours all waved us off while my dad dragged my mother indoors before she caused any more of a scene.

By the time we made it home I could walk again so we got inside quickly. It felt really strange now, when we had left a week ago there were only two of us, now there were three, even if the third one wasn't much bigger than a peanut.

That first night neither of us slept much, every few minutes we were peering into the carry cot, prodding at our new daughter to make sure she was still breathing. She was probably fed up after the first twenty times but she didn't complain. We took turns doing the feeds and the nappies, though every time it was dad's turn to change the nappy the new one fell off as soon as he lifted her up. In his defense, the nappies were far too big for her. I thought we might have to cut some up and make them smaller.

The next day we were exhausted, this was going to take some getting used to. We realized that being parents to a cat doesn't really prepare you for the real thing. For a start, you can't just open the back door and throw a baby outside when it wants to poo. Well you could I suppose but you would soon have Social Services round for a visit.

That first day we both sat looking at her for quite a while. I was thinking about my strange childhood with my even stranger mother. I promised my new daughter that I would never give her a pudding basin haircut or knit her strange clothes and if she ever needed glasses I would make sure they were small and understated, not enormous things with wings and diamantes.

I still stand by the liquorice all-sorts jumper though, she did ask for it and it's not my fault by the time it was finished she had gone off the idea.

I hoped my parent's gene pool had been diluted enough by now that she would grow up relatively normal but still, she also had Frank and Sheila's genes in there somewhere, it was a tough combination to beat.

I was about to voice my concerns to my husband but when I turned around he was already turning to say something to me. We looked at each other and both knew that we were thinking the same thing.

After all we were psychotic.

So, there we were, in three short years I had gone from being a single school leaver serving sausage rolls in a sandwich shop (try saying that fast) to a grown up married mother. How would I cope with this new development?

You'll have to wait and see.

## THE END

Printed in Poland
by Amazon Fulfillment
Poland Sp. z o.o., Wrocław

61035992R00125